A LIVING MINSTRELSY

Sincerely yours,

Sidney Lanier.

"THINE EPITAPH WRIT FAIR IN FRUITAGE ELOQUENT,
THYSELF THY MONUMENT."

A LIVING MINSTRELSY

The
Poetry and Music
of Sidney Lanier

by
JANE S. GABIN

MERCER

ISBN 0-86554-155-8

A *Living Minstrelsy*
Copyright © 1985
Mercer University Press, Macon GA 31207
All rights reserved
Printed in the United States of America

Library of Congress Cataloging in Publication Data
Gabin, Jane S., 1950–
A living minstrelsy
Bibliography: p. 173
Includes index.
1. Lanier, Sidney, 1842–1881. 2. Poets, American—
19th century—Biography. 3. Musicians—United States—
Biography. 4. Music and literature. I. Title.
PS2213.G24   1985   811'.4 [B]   85-5015
ISBN 0-86554-155-8 (alk. paper)

CONTENTS

*For my parents
Billie and Al Gabin
with love*

ACKNOWLEDGMENTS

Many people have made this work an extremely enjoyable project, and I would like to acknowledge their assistance: the staff of the John Work Garrett Library, the Johns Hopkins University, especially Elizabeth Baer, Ben C. Bowman, and Jane Katz; the Special Collections staff of the Milton S. Eisenhower Library, the Johns Hopkins University, especially Carolyn Smith and Carroll Beecheno; the staff of the Willet Memorial Library, Wesleyan College, Macon, Georgia, especially Anne Ledfort and Tena Roberts; Frieda Nadler and Robert C. Quinlan, Macon; and Lester S. Levy, Baltimore.

My thanks also go to Professors Edgar Alden and Daniel Patterson for their guidance; and special thanks belong to Professor Lewis Leary for his encouragement and patience.

And my heartfelt thanks for all his supportiveness belong to my husband and friend, Richard Cramer.

INTRODUCTION

The life of Sidney Lanier is an odyssey from a small Southern city to the great cultural centers of the nation; from a law desk to acknowledged prominence in a major professional orchestra; from an aesthetically restrictive tradition to a life fully imbued with the arts. Throughout his career—from his decision to defy tradition through the years in which he was completely devoted to art—music seems to have been in competition with poetry for his time and attention. But there was never any conflict in the negative sense, for without his musical experiences Lanier could never have written the poetry he was ultimately to create.

Endless frustration, both inspiring and pathetic, distinguishes Sidney Lanier's story. It is a series of thwarted plans, shattered hopes, and incomplete projects. Lanier spent most of his early life dreaming of entering and living within artistic circles, but when he finally decided to devote himself, body and spirit, to attaining this end, he was able to reach only slightly beyond the periphery. He never quite reached his goals. He aimed for the *Atlantic Monthly*, the country's arbiter of literary taste, but reached *Lippincott's*; he vowed to play only for Theodore Thomas's orchestra in New York, but worked with Asger Hamerik at the Peabody Conservatory; he craved acclaim in New York City, but had to settle for Baltimore. True, his accomplishments were of no little consequence—*Lippincott's* was one of the nation's leading publications; Hamerik was a conductor of international reputation; and Baltimore was a thriving and respected center of culture. But they were all second choices for Lanier and represent the disappointment that haunted all of his successes.

Nonetheless, considering Lanier's background, his achievements were almost miraculous. He came from a genteel tradition that scorned the arts as a profession. Feeling that his education was somewhat parochial, he called his college "farcical"; and he had no formal musical training. Constantly hounded by poverty, he was forced to write potboilers, wasting creative energy. He contracted tuberculosis when he was twenty-two, and, by the time he finally determined to pursue an artistic career, he had only seven years to live. Weeks and months of these final years were spent away from his beloved art in a desperate search of a cure.

It is remarkable that Lanier managed to do so much in so little time. He played first flute in a conservatory orchestra and accepted numerous additional musical engagements; delivered popular lectures on Shakespeare and the English novel; developed several essays on music and on literature; wrote a guidebook on Florida which is still popular; wrote children's editions of legendary classics; composed works for voice, piano, and flute; authored one of the best studies of English prosody; and in the midst of all these activities, he wrote dozens of poems, some of which are the most beautifully original in American literature.

His poetic style was his own; the other musical poets of nineteenth-century America, Edgar Allan Poe and Walt Whitman, had little influence on him. Lanier developed his unique style in his own way. A comparison of the early, naive, and sentimental lyrics of *Little Ella* and the intricately textured *Sunrise* illustrates the drastic and revolutionary development of Lanier's poetry.

This evolution was created by the only influence that could have done so—music. It was music that made Lanier a true poet. Without it, his verse would have remained pretty and lyrical, but simple in structure, texturally unimaginative, and tied to a limiting song-concept. But Lanier's best works, written in his last years, reflect the influence of larger musical forms, the blending of voices, lines, and timbres characteristic of the symphony. Lanier's early poems compare to his mature works as Stephen Foster's *Beautiful Dreamer* compares to Liszt's *Mephisto Waltz*. Without his experience with sophisticated orchestral music, Lanier never could have developed as a poet; if he had not played Berlioz's *Symphonie Fantastique*, he might never have written *The Marshes of Glynn*. To Lanier, music and poetry were two different but intimately related media through which to express a single ideal.

Lanier is a unique figure—if not a phenomenon—in American culture. Because he is our only poet who was a professional musician, his poetry is also unique; it is our only poetry whose musical qualities were determined by practical experience. Lanier was an innovator. His work is intriguing, his life inspiring.

CHAPTER I

Macon:
The "Bright Broken Dream"

ON A HOT SUMMER MORNING in 1850, a thin haze floats over the Ocmulgee River as it flows slowly past the young city of Macon, Georgia. Steamboats serving the cotton trade churn the brown waters, pushing beneath the river's eastern bluff. Atop this hill are mysterious Indian mounds, smooth and ancient, but across the river everything is bold and new. The wharves, lined with boats, are faced by shops and warehouses; carts and carriages of merchants trundle the day's wares. Unnoticed, perhaps, a boy of eight moves through the traffic and down to the riverbank where he wanders alone, playing a little flute he has fashioned from a reed. Serene and oblivious, happy with the river and his music, he rambles for hours.

With the years, young Sidney Lanier's reed flute would be replaced by wooden ones, and finally by one made of silver. The boy's simple songs would develop into enchanting melodies, charming ladies in their parlors, soothing prisoners in a war camp, and fascinating audiences in concert halls. His first reveries, with nature and music as his companions, would give way twenty years later to other, deeper dreams, resulting in the creation of some of the most beautiful meditative and lyrical verse in American literature.

Macon, about ninety miles south of Atlanta, was a new town when Lanier was born in 1842; by 1850, its population was still less than six thousand. Its residents were proud of their successful city, which had grown to be a prosperous mercantile center. Lanier's family shared in the general affluence of Macon life; his father had a modest law practice, and his wealthy grandfather owned the large, elegant Lanier House hotel on Mulberry Street. The Lanier home on High Street was a typical middle-class residence—a plain dwelling, rather small, but large enough to contain the refinements of a substantial library and a parlor piano.[1]

As a river port and a railroad center in the 1850s, Macon was a central marketplace for cotton and other farm products. Although the city was more devoted to the growth of its factories and banks than its culture, Wesleyan Female College, the country's first women's college, was founded here in 1839 and the Georgia Academy for the Blind in Macon in 1851. However, there were no public primary schools, and the education of the three Lanier children began—as it did in most Macon families—at home. Sidney was educated in private one-room schools and then at the Bibb County Academy, a small institution founded in 1824 and familiarly called the 'Cademy.[2] Little is known about him as a schoolboy, but he is said to have been a bright, diligent student who enjoyed sports and games such as "cotton merchant," played in a gully near the city's warehouses.

The Lanier home was always filled with music, and, with his mother as instructor, he began piano lessons when he was five. Later, Sidney would listen as she played the piano and "stand by accompanying her on the bones, keeping perfect time."[3] He made his first flute when he was seven, and with this, his younger brother Clifford later recalled, "he sought the woods to emulate the trills and cadences of the song birds."[4] When he later received a one-keyed flute, "much of his leisure was devoted with the passion of a *virtuoso* to practice on this simple flute, on others successively acquired, or on some instrument, piano, violin, organ."[5] When he took

---

[1]Aubrey Harrison Starke, *Sidney Lanier: A Biographical and Critical Study* (reprint, New York: Russell and Russell, 1964) 6.

[2]Ibid., 12.

[3]Mina Mims to Henry W. Lanier, 25 February 1903, Henry W. Lanier Papers, Milton S. Eisenhower Library, the Johns Hopkins University, Baltimore, Maryland.

[4]Clifford A. Lanier, "Sidney Lanier," *Gulf States Historical Magazine* (July 1903): 10.

[5]Clifford A. Lanier, "Reminiscences of Sidney Lanier," *Chautauquan* 21 (July 1895): 405.

up the violin, he would improvise for hours, "entirely oblivious of everything else."[6] His father, however, induced him to give up this instrument—after all, the violin was associated with barrooms! More likely, Robert Lanier feared the alarming transport which violin playing produced in his son and suggested the flute as an alternative. Obediently, Lanier studied the flute and became passionately devoted to it. Throughout Lanier's childhood, music was an important and joyful activity and this elation would never diminish.

What sort of atmosphere did Macon offer a young, creative mind? Lanier's education at the 'Cademy was adequate, but not very intellectually exciting. He found more stimulation investigating the volumes of Scott and Shakespeare in his father's library, learning the language of romance and chivalry from them and not from his lessons. The arts, in general, were not accorded much attention in Macon. Music, except in the church, was considered light entertainment. There were parties and musicales, dances and singing, especially among the young people, but music was not studied seriously, and certainly no gentleman would consider it as a profession.[7] However, it was one of the refined arts taught to the young ladies at the Female Seminary, and some of the ladies even studied singing or piano in New York, as did Lanier's future wife, Mary Day. Society understood music as the province of genteel women and European men; its practice and performance were respectable only when strictly amateur.

The center of cultural activity in Macon was Ralston Hall, a large theater built about 1854 by local businessman James Ralston.[8] Amateur theatricals (including performances of Shakespearean plays), choral concerts, and presentations by visiting artists were given here. Especially popular was an Italian opera company, whose music inspired Lanier's early compositions. Two concerts given in 1858 at Ralston Hall were mentioned in a contemporary history of the city. The first involved a significant element in American musical life, the "traveling virtuosi." Macon was vis-

---

[6]Mina Mims to Henry W. Lanier, 25 February 1903, Henry W. Lanier Papers, Milton S. Eisenhower Library.

[7]Gilbert Chase, *America's Music: From the Pilgrims to the Present*, rev. 2d ed. (New York: McGraw-Hill, 1966) 341.

[8]John C. Butler, *Historical Record of Macon and Central Georgia* (Macon: J. W. Burke, 1879) 204.

ited by pianist Sigismund Thalberg, who appealed to his audiences with his keyboard pyrotechnics, and Belgian violinist Henri Vieuxtemps; they played before "a very large and brilliant audience." And in March, the Young America Ballet Corps played a three-day engagement, "presenting a pageant never before witnessed in the city, and carried the vast audience every night by storm."[9] Other than these rare events and the amateur recitals given by the young ladies, there was very little music in Macon.

In 1857, when Lanier was fifteen, he entered Oglethorpe University, a small Presbyterian school located a few miles from Milledgeville, then Georgia's capital. Being an apt scholar, he was admitted as a sophomore. Robert Lanier chose Oglethorpe for his son because he felt that the school would provide Sidney with a foundation in the classics in an atmosphere of strong adherence to religious faith. The school was isolated from town life and afforded its students an "essentially primitive"[10] existence virtually devoid of frivolous distractions. In later years, Lanier called his college "farcical"[11]; even while a student, he told his father that he gained more from discussions with friends in their secret literary society—the Thalian Society—than from his classes.

Although he studied mathematics, Greek and Latin, philosophy, and science, Lanier found time for his flute. His friends recalled the magic of his music-making. "Sid would play upon his flute like one inspired while the rest of us would listen in solemn silence." His roommate T. F. Newell told how Lanier would "extemporize the sweetest music ever vouchsafed to mortal ear."[12] Another companion, J. O. Varnedoe, noted that music, "rather than intellectual affinity, was the potent influence that determined the choice of his comrades."[13]

---

[9]Ibid., 215.

[10]Edwin Mims, *Sidney Lanier* (New York: Houghton, Mifflin, 1905) 26.

[11]Sidney Lanier, "To Robert S. Lanier," 29 November 1873, in *The Centennial Edition of the Works of Sidney Lanier*, ed. Charles R. Anderson et al., 10 vols. (Baltimore: Johns Hopkins Press, 1945) 8:423 (hereafter cited as CE).

[12]Quoted in Mims, *Sidney Lanier*, 32-33.

[13]Quoted in Starke, *Sidney Lanier*, 27.

Lanier read voraciously and especially enjoyed Shakespeare, the Romantic poets, and idealistic tales evoking the spirit of medieval chivalry. His apparent favorite among the poets was Tennyson (all of Lanier's extant songs, with the exception of *Little Ella*, are musical settings of Tennyson's lyrics). In the essays of Thomas Carlyle he found many ideas to which he was receptive—especially that of the intertwining of music and poetry. More important, Carlyle introduced Lanier to German literature, initiating his intense interest in the works of Richter, Novalis, and Heine. Here he found a world of drama, romance, and poetic heroes. This fascination with German culture was crystallized by his friendship with Professor James Woodrow, whom he met his senior year.

Woodrow provided Lanier with an intellectual bent and saved Lanier's education from being totally parochial. The professor, a native of England, had emigrated to Pennsylvania as a child and had come to Georgia after studying at Harvard and the university at Heidelberg, Germany. He was a liberal natural scientist and minister who would eventually be condemned for heresy by the General Assembly of the Presbyterian Church for his belief in evolution.[14] Woodrow encouraged the young man's academic inclinations and, after Lanier's graduation in 1860 as one of two valedictorians, had him appointed as a tutor at Oglethorpe. Their friendship deepened as Lanier accompanied the professor on his preaching circuit. Long talks during these rides awakened within Lanier ideas about religion, science, and scholarship; he began to nurture a dream of going to Heidelberg himself, to emerge from the university there as scholar and professor.

Left to his own sense of obligation, Lanier would perhaps have gone to Heidelberg, or at least pursued an academic life at home. Music was not a goal, for although he loved it deeply he realized it could not be a life's work: "the prime inclination—that is, natural bent (which I have checked, though) of my nature is to music. . . . I cannot bring myself to believe that I was intended for a musician, because it seems so small a business in comparison with other things which, it seems to me, I might do." Then he asked himself, "What is the province of music in the economy of the world?"[15] He resolved the question—at least for the moment—and turned

---

[14]Mims, *Sidney Lanier*, 28-29.

[15]Quoted in ibid., 38-39.

his concentration upon his responsibilities at Oglethorpe—lecturing, debating, watching over his freshman brother, and devouring German classics.

However, other plans were being made for the future of young men like Sidney Lanier. In January 1861, Georgia seceded from the Union. In April, Fort Sumter was bombarded. In July, Sidney Lanier enlisted in the Macon Volunteers, one of twenty-six companies from the city. He was not eager for a civil war, but was ready to answer the call of his state and defend its withdrawal. Adventure was also promised, adventure like that in the great novels of chivalry. There was excitement in the streets of Milledgeville and Macon, for the winds of war, as Lanier later wrote, "thundered splendidly in the impassioned appeals of orators. . . . it stole in to the firesides, it clinked glasses in bar-rooms, it lifted the gray hairs of our wise men in conventions, it thrilled through the lectures in college halls, it rustled the thumbed book-leaves of the school-rooms."[16] The horrors of war were not yet anticipated. Only when it was over could Lanier reflect that one of the causes of the conflict was the egotism of the whole nation: "this perpetual arrogant invitation to draw and come on: this eternal posture of insult in which we walked about with our clenched fist thrust in the faces of all nations."[17]

But in 1861 the war, to Lanier, was a challenge, an exercise in chivalry. He packed his "Zauberflöte" and several volumes of poetry with his soldier's gear, for there would likely be ample opportunity for playing and reading since much of his company's duty would be guarding the Carolina and Virginia beaches. It was not taxing duty and leisure hours were plentiful; Lanier attended officers' dinners, participated in a "little sociable," and serenaded the ladies of the towns where they were stationed.

Lanier's flute served him well. One evening, he and several comrades serenaded the ladies of Petersburg, Virginia, and "went back to . . . our quarters laden with bouquets." On another occasion when he played beneath the windows of a music club in one small town, the musicians came down to listen to him and gave him "the honorary freedom of the town." In another village, Lanier went into a music store, asked for a flute, and

---

[16]*Tiger-Lilies*, CE, 5:96.

[17]Lanier, "Bombs From Below: Wanted, Engineers!" CE, 5:204.

when he played it, "the delighted and charmed proprietor insisted upon presenting it to him."[18]

Lanier was fortunate; he was never wounded and, except for duty at Chancellorsville and the "seven-days battle" near Richmond, he saw little combat. In the summer of 1862, he was transferred to the Signal Corps and was stationed across the James River from Newport News, near Fort Boykin. Here he met General John Hankins, who lived near the fort in a seventeenth-century manor house. Lanier visited the family for serenades and lively discussions of literature. He became "firm Soul-friends" with the general's daughter Virginia, to whom he wrote many romantic letters in the following months, calling her "Meine Heiss-geliebte."[19] He was also writing Mary Day of Macon, whom he had met while at home on a short leave, addressing her as "Du Himmel's Liebchen."[20] Lanier was "always in love,"[21] and the excitement of the war added to the atmosphere of romance. The war seemed full of dash and gallantry, "largely a picnic—a holiday time it was—'the gay days of mandolin and guitar and moonlight sails on the James River.' "[22]

Lanier's luck held almost to the end of the war, when he lost all of his books to a Union raiding party. "For long thenceforth," recalled Clifford, "we were sadly lacking underwear, and sadly bewailed our want of high Dutch poetry, French rhetoric, English blank verse, and American sentimentalism."[23] In the summer of 1864, Lanier saw service as a signal officer aboard a blockade-runner that ran from Wilmington, North Carolina, to the West Indies. In November, his ship, the *Lucy*, was captured by a Union steamer, and Lanier was sent to a prisoner-of-war camp at Point Lookout, Maryland. It is said that Lanier hid his flute up the sleeve of his uniform to prevent its confiscation by Union soldiers, and he was able to

---

[18]Aubrey Harrison Starke, "Sidney Lanier as a Musician," *Musical Quarterly* 20 (October 1934): 386.

[19]Lanier, "To Virginia Hankins," 28 July 1864, CE, 7:158.

[20]Lanier, "To Mary Day," 12 April 1864, ibid., 148.

[21]Starke, *Sidney Lanier*, 51.

[22]Mims, *Sidney Lanier*, 48.

[23]Clifford A. Lanier, "Reminiscences of Sidney Lanier," 408.

take it into prison with him. Amid the deathly conditions under which the twelve thousand men were confined, it was a source of comfort.

Among those who found solace in Lanier's music was John Banister Tabb, a young Virginian who had also been captured while trying to run the blockade. Later, Tabb recalled his first meeting with the prisoner from Georgia in the "hell-hole" of Point Lookout: "One day, while I was lying in my cot, ill with fever, the distant notes of a flute reached my ears from the opposite side of the camp. I was entranced. I said to myself, 'I must find that man.' As soon as I got out of bed I commenced searching, with the result that I found the flutist in the poet Sidney Lanier. From that happy moment until my release we spent the time together. We became fast friends and always remained such."[24]

Lanier and Tabb, who compared their friendship to that of David and Jonathan, were kindred spirits, united by a love of literature and music; they would often spend their evenings at Point Lookout in discussion. Tabb also had had an affinity for music since childhood; therefore when news reached Lanier just after the war that Tabb had gone to Baltimore for piano studies, he wrote: "I'm just *infinitely* glad you're studying Music . . . and hope yet to hear you play. Study *Chopin* as soon as you become able to play his music: and get his 'life,' by *Liszt*."[25] However, the two men did not see each other again until 1877.[26]

Although Lanier was kept at Point Lookout for only three months, it was enough to destroy his health; when he left, he was afflicted with tuberculosis. From the time of his capture, he had hoped to be released in an exchange of prisoners, but his freedom was not obtained until February 1865 and then only through the influence of some gold smuggled into the

---

[24]Quoted in Francis A. Litz, *Father Tabb* (Baltimore: Johns Hopkins Press, 1923) 23-24.

[25]Lanier, "To John B. Tabb," 20 January 1867, CE, 7:262-63.

[26]There is not a great deal of primary information on this relationship, for most of Lanier's letters to Tabb were destroyed in a fire in 1911, and Tabb did not wish his own correspondence published. But the existing evidence indicates that their friendship was warm and sincere, and also that Lanier helped Tabb by criticizing his poems, aiding in their publication, and, ultimately, by influencing Tabb's style. Tabb paid a personal tribute to Lanier in his work, dedicating to him his 1894 *Poems*, in addition to several individual works.

prison by a friend. He was transported by ship to City Point, Virginia, and his "Zauberflöte" again played a crucial role in his fate.

The ship was locked in the frozen harbor; down in the hold, Lanier lay ill, almost to the point of death. A fellow soldier was playing Lanier's flute when the commanding officer of the ship and his wife were visited by Mrs. Mattie Montgomery of Alabama and her young daughter Ella. They were family friends of the Laniers, but were unaware that Sidney was on board. When the child heard the music drifting from the hold, she called down to ask who had been playing. The soldier who replied said that the flute's owner was too sick to answer, that he would probably die, and that his name was Sidney Lanier. It was indeed her "Brother Sid"! Lanier was carried up from the hold, warmed and fed. He asked for his flute, and as he began to play softly, a "yell of joy came up from the shivering wretches down below, who knew that their comrade was alive."[27] Finally, Lanier was released from the ship and began his long journey home.

It took Lanier a month to get to Macon; he had to make most of the journey on foot, which aggravated his already weakened condition. When he arrived in March he was shocked by the transformation that had taken place in his city. The gentle life he remembered was obliterated. Now the city was filled with refugees; supplies were low; schools had been turned into hospitals; many of Lanier's friends and classmates had been killed or wounded.

But Macon had been luckier than most Southern cities. Its homes were crowded with refugees after the fall of Atlanta and provided safety until July 1864, when Federal raids began. Macon was spared from Sherman's march when Union troops descended on the capital, Milledgeville, instead. Finally, with too few men for defense and too little food, Macon was surrendered on 20 April 1865.

There was no more music in the Lanier home. Sidney was seriously ill, having collapsed as soon as he had returned. And his mother was dying of consumption; she only wanted to see her two sons home from the war. Clifford, whose blockade runner had been unable to return to the Carolina coast, had sailed to Cuba and then Texas; he walked from Galveston

---

[27]Mims, *Sidney Lanier*, 60-62.

to Macon. Clifford arrived on 19 May, and Mrs. Lanier died three days later.

Life in all its aspects had changed for the family. Robert Lanier had never been wealthy, but now he had nothing. The fortunes of Grandfather Lanier had been virtually destroyed. It was obvious that the dreams fostered during Sidney Lanier's college days could not be realized, for now he had to spend what little strength he had to earn a living, locking him in the double vise of poverty and illness; he had to work in order to live, but he was often too sick to work. In the summer of 1865, he worked as a tutor in a plantation home near Macon, but in October he moved to Point Clear on Mobile Bay in Alabama for the sake of his health. He thought "the Gulf Coast might avert the Consumption which threatens me."[28] Lanier was extremely depressed about his health: "My destitute condition is the Death's Head at all my feasts," he wrote to Clifford. "Two months more, like the two months gone, will put me yonder beside Mother—. To which, personally, I don't know that I would have much objection: being deeply convinced that nothing could exceed the unceasing sufferings that I endure all the time in secret."[29]

Clifford was working as a clerk in the Exchange Hotel in Montgomery, Alabama, and in the winter his older brother joined him. Sidney did not totally neglect his artistic inclinations during this time; he wrote several songs (*Song of Elaine* and *Little Ella*, dedicated to the child who had discovered him on the prison ship, date from this period), continued writing his war novel, and collaborated with Clifford on poetry. But he resented having to spend most of his time and strength at unrewarding work. "Necessity has driven a wedge into my life, and split it in two," he wrote. "Whereas I *used* to live wholly to make beautiful things, I *now* live *half-ly* to make *money*: and I hate all half-way things, and so I don't like to talk about it."[30] But life in Montgomery was not completely devoid of culture: there was a literary society to which the Lanier brothers belonged and amateur musicales in which they participated; Sidney also obtained a position as organist of the Presbyterian church.

---

[28]Lanier, "To Virginia Hankins," 15 November 1865, CE, 7:207.

[29]November 1865, ibid., 208.

[30]Lanier, "To Harriet (Freeman) Fulton," 22 January 1866, ibid., 211.

In the early spring, his health improved, Lanier returned to Macon with the manuscript of his completed philosophical-romantic Civil War novel, *Tiger-Lilies*. After a short visit, he went to New York in search of a publisher. He stayed a month, exploring the city, meeting the Northern Laniers for the first time, and planning a whole variety of "projects." He attended numerous concerts, sure that "so far, I can beat all to pieces any flutist I've heard." He hoped for a position with the "Literary Bureau," contemplated delivering "a lecture for the Southern Relief," and considered "getting together a 'flute orchestra' and airing the same in Steinway Hall."[31] But none of these projects materialized; even his primary objective was not successful. Although he was able to find a publisher for *Tiger-Lilies*, Sidney had to pay to have it printed.

Returning to Macon for the summer, Lanier was soon involved in serious personal decisions. Mary Day, who had been engaged during the war and had rejected Lanier's suit at the time, was now free and allowed a renewal of their correspondence. With the Laniers and the Days boarding at Wesleyan College, Sidney had the opportunity to see her again. Their friendship deepened, and by the summer of 1867 they were engaged; their marriage took place that December.

There remained, however, the question of Sidney's career. At this point, he still clung to the hope of finding some sort of academic position and applied at the University of Alabama. He hoped that his forthcoming novel, which "contains some popularized metaphysical discussions . . . might assist towards an estimate of my fitness for the Chair of Philosophy."[32] He was awarded no such position, and his plans to teach at Oakland College in Mississippi were also thwarted because of the school's poor financial condition. He was, however, offered the principalship of the Prattville Academy, a small school about twenty miles from Montgomery; he assumed the position in September 1867. But the desire to teach at a large university never dimmed; it was a hope that Lanier was to nurture for another decade. He was to lecture on Shakespeare at the Peabody Institute in Baltimore in 1878, but did not obtain a long-desired lectureship at the Johns Hopkins University until 1879.

---

[31]Lanier, "To Clifford A. Lanier," April 1867, ibid., 281.

[32]Lanier, "To Virginia Clay," 6 August 1867, ibid., 305.

Before leaving for Prattville, Lanier took part in the renewed musical activity in Macon and joined the Musical Society. He also appeared in two concerts at Ralston Hall. The first, held 19 June 1867, was billed as a "Grand Concert!" Lanier played *La Favorite de Vienne* by Terschak and an original solo composition (which apparently does not survive) entitled *Le Ruisseau.*[33] Other pieces on the program, mostly excerpts from Italian opera, showed that Macon's musical tastes had changed little in a decade. The Italian school still ruled, and the newer German music, already arrived in New York, had not yet drifted South.

Macon was proud of Lanier, as was revealed in a notice of the concert appearing in the Macon *Telegraph* on the morning of the performance:

> We wish we had space to speak of Mr. Lanier's wonderful musical talent. He is an author and a poet; but not alone with his pen does he unburden his soul. The poetical utterances of his flute address themselves to every sentimental nature, and thrill with exquisite pleasure. He makes his flute rival the most effective and emotional instrument—the violin—and that bespeaks for him a gift and a power in execution that is certainly remarkable. He will perform a concerted piece, with one of the Professors, but we trust he will not withhold one of his own weird improvisations.[34]

Even in this very early critique—probably written by one of Macon's genteel enthusiasts whose opinions were likely based more on admiration for Lanier than on musical expertise—there are two words that would recur frequently in succeeding reviews by more sophisticated correspondents: "poetical" and "emotional." Lanier's compositions were almost always described fervidly by reviewers who attended his concerts. The rationale for this does not seem to lie so much in composition, but in performance; Lanier's virtuosic playing technique transformed these pieces into arresting, exquisite works. And always, there was the intense emotionality of his playing—from his childhood reveries, to the "trance-like state" into which he fell while playing the flute at college, to the tenderness which made imprisoned soldiers weep—that gave his pieces their singular quality.

---

[33]Concert program, Charles D. Lanier Collection, Milton S. Eisenhower Library, the Johns Hopkins University, Baltimore, Maryland.

[34]Macon *Telegraph*, 19 June 1867.

Other performers in the 19 June concert were two Macon ladies, Mrs. Augusta Lamar Ogden and her cousin Mrs. Virginia Lamar Bacon. The "Professors" mentioned in the newspaper joined Lanier, Ogden, and Bacon in another concert in Ralston Hall on 28 June; they were Professor Vincent Czurda of Wesleyan Female College, and a Professor Kueringer. The program again consisted largely of pieces from the Italian school, and Lanier contributed his *Fife and Bugle* and *Swamp Robin*, neither of which is extant.[35]

In the fall of 1867, Lanier went to Prattville, but his work there was far from rewarding. The climate was inhospitable, and that winter he suffered a pulmonary hemorrhage—an irrefutable symptom of tuberculosis. At the end of the school year Prattville Academy was closed and the Laniers, who had been married for six months, returned to Georgia. There now seemed only one solution to the question of a career for Lanier—to study law and enter practice with his father. Lanier accepted this duty, but did not, and could never, embrace it.

Something was missing from his life in Macon. The musical opportunities that existed offered no challenge and could not compensate for the lack of excitement he found in his work. Concerts were designed to please everyone, and entertainment rather than aesthetic taste was the controlling principle. A typical concert at Ralston Hall in 1869, this one to benefit St. Paul's Church, offered a mixture of Beethoven's *Egmont* overture, Gottschalk's *Last Hope*, *Come Where My Love Lies Dreaming* by Stephen Foster, and a selection of pieces by various composers—Schubert, Donizetti, and Ambroise Thomas as well as several composers now forgotten.[36] Music was still reserved for small recitals, public occasions such as when "Prof. Sidney Lanier" (who was apparently "Prof." only for this event) played "Sacred Melodies" at the 1868 exercises of the Adelphean Society at Wesleyan, and for courting, as Lanier and Mary Day had, playing duets in the college parlor. Anything approaching professionalism in music had to be sought elsewhere, and Lanier knew this.

His old dreams of a life of art, which an occasional amateur musicale could not satisfy, were aroused. In the days immediately after the war, La-

---

[35]CE, 6:389-90.

[36]Original concert program, 25 November 1869, Charles D. Lanier Papers, John Work Garrett Library, the Johns Hopkins University, Baltimore, Maryland.

nier's major concern was staying alive; he knew he was very ill, and the prospect of drudging at unrewarding work, trammeled by necessity, when there was so much else he wanted to do, was frightening. He knew that life meant more than simply sustaining one's physical needs. His work did nothing for his spiritual needs; these could be served only by art. But a sense of duty—and the hold of tradition—kept him at his law desk. He would ultimately rebel, but it would take him several years to make a final break with the old life.

CHAPTER II

The Decision

THE YEARS FROM 1869 TO 1873 brought Lanier anxiety, suffering, and intermittent bursts of hope. He spent this time shuttling between his law desk in Macon and various refuges—in Georgia, Tennessee, Virginia, and Texas—in vain attempts to find relief from his illness. When he was not ill, he was poring over law books; there seemed to be no question of his not working, for now he had a family to support. But a happy family life is the only thing that saved him from succumbing to depression. Intellectually, he was growing and was able to call the novel, which he had once hoped would win him an academic position, a "foolish book . . . of a foolish boy," and exclaim, "Ah, how I have outgrown Tiger Lilies in these two years."[1]

He did not receive incentives from within Macon, but only when his fortunes—or lack of them—took him to New York. Lanier had had a brief taste of the city in 1867, but when he returned in April 1869 on business for his father's law firm, he had the leisure to enjoy some of the cultural offerings around him. On 28 April, soon after his arrival, he attended a performance at the Grand Opera House. His reactions, little changed from his undergraduate musical ecstasies, are effusive: "As the fair, tender notes came, they opened . . . like flower-buds expanding into flowers under the sweet rain of the accompaniment: Kind Heaven! My head fell on the seat

---

[1]Sidney Lanier, "To Virginia Hankins," 17 May 1869, in *The Centennial Edition of the Works of Sidney Lanier*, ed. Charles R. Anderson et al., 10 vols. (Baltimore: Johns Hopkins Press, 1945) 8:31 (hereafter cited as CE).

in front, I was utterly weighed down with great loves and great ideas. . . . *I also lived these flower-tone lives.*"² But his reaction to *La Belle Hélène* at the Fifth Avenue Theatre evoked no such raptures: "The gestures, the music, the songs, were all infinitely lascivious and suggestive. . . . I am sick that music is fallen into such hands and gone to serve such passions."³ Here his Puritan side, so often at war with his Cavalier exuberance, kept him from enjoying the music; but he was aware that he was hearing professional performances, something he could not get at home.

A third visit to New York took place late in the summer of 1870, this time for medical reasons. Swedish physician Dr. E. E. Marcy offered Lanier treatment for his bronchial "obstruction," filling Lanier once again with the hope of a cure. The treatment proved futile, and only the company of friends and an occasional taste of good music kept his spirits alive. In New York, wrote Lanier, there were "no streams,—save of sin—and no fine airs,—save those of Theo. Thomas' Orchestra."⁴ On 8 August, he attended the opening-night concert of Thomas's orchestra—the most significant musical ensemble in the city—at Central Park Garden, where "the dear flutes and oboes and horns drifted me hither and thither, and the great violins and small violins swayed me upon waves and overflowed me."⁵

The next week he made further strides in his growing musical sophistication when he heard Wagner for the first time, although the composer's music had been in America for a decade. He was aware of Wagner and had admired him as being representative of the German culture he loved so well. "Ah, how they have belied Wagner!" he cried to his wife about the controversial composer. "I heard Theo. Thomas' Orchestra play his overture to Tannhäuser. The 'Music of the Future' is surely thy music and my music. . . . The sequences flowed along, one after the other, as if all the great and noble deeds of time had formed a procession and marched in review before one's *ears*, instead of one's eyes. . . . I would I might lead a so magnificent file of glories into Heaven!"⁶

---

²Lanier, "To Mary Day Lanier," 28 April 1869, CE, 8:17.

³Lanier, "To Mary Day Lanier," 1 May 1869, ibid., 19.

⁴Lanier, "To Mary Day Lanier," 7 August 1870, ibid., 91.

⁵Lanier, "To Mary Day Lanier," 8 August 1870, ibid., 92.

⁶15 August 1870, ibid., 99.

In late September, Lanier returned to Macon, but he was still quite ill. He could practice law only in spurts, for he spent much of the winter traveling, searching for a climate milder than that of Macon. A year later, in the fall of 1871, he was back in New York at Marcy's office, again with hope. The doctor was certain that medication and a "lifting cure" would relieve his patient. Apparently Lanier was in accord with Marcy, for his letters to his family at this time reflect his improved spirits and physical progress. However, in the nineteenth century, tuberculosis was a mystery disease, and a cure was never achieved.

But the atmosphere of the city was like a tonic to him. The day after his arrival, Lanier wrote to his wife: "I am just going out to Theo. Thomas'. There are only two more nights before he closes for the season, and I cannot resist the temptation to drink a little of this Wine-of-Heaven."[7] The Puritan in Lanier made him see the city as a "wicked Babylon," but the rest of him, his pleasure-loving side, enjoyed good dinners, the autumn sunshine, and the city's abundant cultural offerings.

Lanier remained a passive participant in the musical life of New York. It was only after his experiences during the winter of 1872-1873 that he was able to return to the city and play a somewhat active role. In November 1872, the "lifting cure" and all other supposed cures having been of no use, Lanier journeyed to San Antonio, Texas, hoping to find relief in its drier climate. What he found was more beneficial than the weather. Lanier located a large community of immigrant Germans, which included many musicians. Here he was finally living, as an active participant, in an environment that was not only hospitable to professional musicianship, but one that encouraged it. At last he was able to receive recognition for his musical gifts from people to whom music was not a gentlemanly adornment, but an essential component of life.

He could discuss his beloved German literature, spend long evenings in convivial conversation, and for the first time indulge himself wholly in musical activity. The first evening that he was taken to the practice session of the Männerchor he was so moved by their *lieder* that "imperious tears rushed into my eyes, I could scarce restrain myself from running and kissing each one in turn and from howling dolefully the while."[8] Later in

---

[7]Lanier, "To Mary Day Lanier," 21 September 1871, ibid., 177.

[8]Lanier, "To Mary Day Lanier," 1 January 1873, ibid., 320.

the evening Lanier was asked to play the flute, and somewhat miraculously he found his powers improved, either because of regained health or confidence from his sympathetic environment, or, most likely, a combination of both. "To my utter astonishment, I was perfect master of the instrument. Is not this most strange? . . . I *certainly* have not practiced: and yet there I commanded and the blessed notes obeyed me, and when I had finished, amid a storm of applause . . . I played once more during the evening: and indeed with even more rapturous bravos than before. . . . I also feel better today than in a long time."[9]

Lanier continued his musical activities in San Antonio, and a month after his first appearance with the Männerchor, his emotions were still in a heightened state. He reported that his soul "hath been cutting swiftly into the great space of the Subtle Unspeakable Deep, driven by wind after wind of heavenly melody,"[10] and that although "Ineffable poems,—of music and of words—torment me, I have not the patience enough for a pen."[11]

Although no poems were written during the San Antonio period, Lanier immersed himself in musical composition. He had already worked at songwriting, producing his sentimental ballad *Little Ella* in 1866, and he had set several lyrics of Tennyson to music: *Song of Elaine* probably in 1862, and *Flow Down, Cold Rivulet, Love That Hath Us in the Net*, and *Break, Break, Break* probably in 1871.[12] His several concert appearances after the war and before his going to San Antonio featured others of his original compositions, but none of these have ever been located. In Texas, he returned to composition with increased powers of musical perception.

Lanier's first attempts at music writing in San Antonio were brief. A fragmentary piece entitled *Wind-Song* antedates the later, four-page solo composition for flute, which Lanier was to play before Leopold Damrosch in New York in 1873. On the same sheet of manuscript paper are four other very short studies: *The song of the lost spirit, Heimweh Polka, Bird Song*, and

---

[9]Ibid., 320-21.

[10]Lanier, "To Mary Day Lanier," 24 February 1873, ibid., 332.

[11]Lanier, "To Mary Day Lanier," 25 February 1873, ibid.

[12]Richard Higgins, "Sidney Lanier, Musician" (dissertation, Peabody Conservatory of Music, 1969).

Condilicatezza.[13] These fragments, with the exception of *Wind-Song* and *Bird Song*—indications of Lanier's consistent desire to capture the sounds of nature with his flute—are of little interest; neither do they appear to have aroused any fervor in their creator.

At the end of February 1873, he wrote triumphantly of a new composition: "I have writ the most beautiful piece,—'Field-larks and Black-birds,' wherein I have mirrored Mons. Field-lark's pretty eloquence so that I doubt he wd. know the difference betwixt the flute and his own voice."[14] There is no piece with this title among Lanier's extant music manuscripts, though there is a second page of a composition headed "Black-birds." It was his execution of *Black-birds* that first earned Lanier the admiration of Asger Hamerik of the Peabody Institute.

It was important that Lanier received popular acclaim as a musician, but it was crucial that the exultation he now derived from playing and composing made him finally realize that his life could be fulfilled only through music. The safety of a law practice in Macon could never drive him into the "sacred frenzy" that music inspired. Aubrey Starke points out the irony that San Antonio, which was supposed to have offered Lanier rest and health, gave him a "taste of success."[15] With the possibility of a musical career even vaguely, distantly waved before his face, Lanier could not be complacent. He determined to go north and pursue an artistic career.

The succeeding months were spent in preparation and conflict. Deterrents to Lanier's dream were his health, family responsibilities, and financial problems. Edwin Mims notes that Lanier's resolve "is all the more significant when it is remembered that the year 1873 was one of financial distress, especially in the South."[16] In addition, by pursuing music as a career, Lanier would be acting contrary to genteel Southern tradition. But, as he told Clifford, "An impulse, simply irresistible, drives me into the

---

[13]Manuscript, Henry W. Lanier Papers, John Work Garrett Library, the Johns Hopkins University, Baltimore, Maryland.

[14]Lanier, "To Mary Day Lanier," 28 February 1873, CE, 8:335.

[15]Aubrey Harrison Starke, *Sidney Lanier: A Biographical and Critical Study* (reprint, New York: Russell and Russell, 1964) 163.

[16]Edwin Mims, *Sidney Lanier* (New York: Houghton, Mifflin, 1905) 123.

world of poetry and music." And a letter to his father, written four months later, after Lanier was already in New York, reveals the anguish and courage that forged his decision:

> My dear father, think how, for twenty years, through poverty, through pain, through weariness, through sickness, through the uncongenial atmospheres of a farcical college and of a bare army and then of an exacting business-life, through all the discouragement of being born on the wrong side of Mason-and-Dickson's [sic] line and of being wholly unacquainted with literary people and literary ways,—I say, think how, in spite of all these depressing circumstances and of a thousand more which I could enumerate, these two figures of music and of poetry have steadily kept in my heart, so that I could not banish them! Does it not seem to you, as to me, that I begin to have the right to enroll myself among the devotees of these two sublime arts, after having followed them so long and so humbly and through so much bitterness?[17]

But it was music that chiefly motivated Lanier. Starke points out two major evidences of this: the fact that none of Lanier's published poems seem to have been written in 1872 or 1873; and Lanier's letter to his friend, Southern poet Paul Hamilton Hayne.[18] He wrote that "so much of my life consists of music. . . . whatever turn I have for Art, is purely musical; poetry being, with me, a mere tangent into which I shoot sometimes. I could play passably on several instruments before I could write legibly: and since then, the very deepest of my life has been filled with music, which I have studied and cultivated far more than poetry."[19]

Now, however, with Clifford assuming the financial care of his wife and children, Sidney was free to pursue his musical fortune in the city that was the aspiration of every serious musician in America: New York. But on the way, he made a crucial stop in Baltimore.

Lanier stopped over in Baltimore to visit a friend, Henry Wysham, who was also a lawyer and flute player. Wysham enjoyed a position of some eminence in Baltimore, having played with such organizations as the Liederkranz orchestra, and was now first flute in the Peabody Institute

---

[17]Lanier, "To Robert S. Lanier," 29 November 1873, CE, 8:423-24.

[18]Starke, *Sidney Lanier*, 164.

[19]26 May 1873, CE, 8:347.

orchestra.[20] On the afternoon of 22 September 1873, Lanier visited Wysham at his home at 102 East Madison Street, just three blocks from the Peabody's impressive building on Mount Vernon Place. Wysham also invited Asger Hamerik, the Danish conductor of the orchestra, for the express purpose of hearing Lanier play. The result of this informal audition, at which Lanier played his *Black-birds*, was Hamerik's offer of the position of first flute in the soon-to-be-organized full Peabody orchestra. Hamerik, wrote Lanier to Mary, "expressed himself in such approval as would have delighted thy loving heart beyond measure. He declared the composition to be that of an Artist, and the playing to be almost perfect, with a grave and manifestly hearty manner which could not be mistaken." To his father, Lanier wrote that Hamerik "offered me the position of first flute . . . at the same time expressing himself in the most marked manner, both upon the style of my composition, and my playing."[21]

Could Lanier have been exaggerating Hamerik's enthusiasm, possibly mingling it with his own and thereby magnifying it? There is a thread of possibility in this, especially since, in the same letters, Lanier is overcome with excitement and refers to Hamerik as "one of the most accomplished composers and *Maestros* in the world" and "one who is regarded (he is so spoken of in one of the musical papers of this city) as a composer just below the Classic Beethoven & Mozart, whose compositions are played along with those of the great masters."[22] Hamerik's contemporary reputation was very good, though Lanier might have been indulging in hyperbole. A possible motive for this might have been his continual need to represent music as an honorable profession, especially to his conservative father.

There are two strong points of evidence that indicate that Hamerik was sincere in his enthusiastic appraisal of Lanier. The first is that he gave Lanier a letter of recommendation, written right then in Wysham's library, to Theodore Thomas. If Hamerik had been hesitant about Lanier's talents, it is doubtful that he, who was trying to establish a reputation and an orchestra on a par with Thomas, would have affixed his name to such

---

[20]Lubov Keefer, *Baltimore's Music: The Haven of the American Composer* (Baltimore: J. H. Furst, 1962) 116 n.7.

[21]24 September 1873, CE, 8:388, 384-85.

[22]Ibid., 384, 388.

a letter. There is also Hamerik's own later evaluation of Lanier as a musician: "In his hands the flute no longer remained a mere material instrument, but was transformed into a voice that set heavenly harmonies into vibration. Its tone developed colors, warmth, and a low sweetness of unspeakable poetry. His playing appealed alike to the musically learned and to the unlearned—for he would magnetize the listener; but the artist felt in his performance the superiority of the momentary living inspiration to all the rules and shifts of mere technical scholarship. His art was not only the art of art, but an art above art."[23]

Still glowing from his interview with Hamerik, Lanier arrived at his destination—New York—in late September 1873. At last he was entering the city as a musician, cherishing the hope that through his diligence and skill he might play with Thomas's orchestra.

When Lanier arrived in New York, it was a city of almost a million people and was growing rapidly. The streets of lower Manhattan were already so crowded that an arcade railway was being contemplated, and one experimental stretch of subway had been built. The "Tweed Ring" scandal had just shaken politics, and the city's new leaders were striving for reforms. Life appeared prosperous. The streets were thronged with horsecars and shoppers; the stores were stocked with goods from around the world; the hotels were filled with guests arriving at the piers or at the newly opened Grand Central Station. But difficult times were not far distant. The Panic of 1873, which was to sweep the entire nation, began on Wall Street in September. It was a poor time for a man to try to make his fortune in New York.

However, the cultural life of the city was flourishing, and from this aspect Lanier came to New York at an advantageous time. The arts were flowering as never before, attested to by the recent opening of the Metropolitan Museum of Art.[24] New York was also the center of America's music. It had more musical organizations, more musical journals, and more concerts than any other city in the country. The orchestra was enjoying its first real glory, in most part due to the efforts of Theodore Thomas.

---

[23]Quoted in Mims, *Sidney Lanier*, 132.

[24]I. N. Phelps Stokes, *New York Past and Present* (New York: Plantin Press, 1939) 48-49.

Working as conductor of an opera orchestra, Thomas realized that the city needed more music and founded his own orchestra in 1862. By the end of the Civil War, his ensemble and its concert series were fixtures in the city's cultural life. Thomas gave "Unrivalled Summer Night's Concerts" in Central Park Garden, and later took the orchestra on tour to major American cities, bringing new music to wide sections of the country.[25]

Opera in New York was also given new vitality and professionalism in 1873 when James Henry Mapleson, a leading English impresario who worked with such renowned singers as Adelina Patti, Clara Louise Kellogg, Christine Nilsson, Lillian Nordica, and Francesco Tomagno, came to conduct his company at the Academy of Music on Fourteenth Street. There were also smaller theaters where both professional and amateur operatic productions were presented. Chamber concerts and solo recitals abounded, and European artists visited constantly. In 1870, Lanier had heard violinist Henri Vieuxtemps, and in 1873 he heard the Polish composer-violinist Henryk Wieniawski, both at Steinway Hall in New York.

Upon his arrival in New York, Lanier quickly became involved in its musical life and began to attract notice. According to Aubrey Starke, critics gave auditions to Lanier, and leading musicians "spent whole afternoons playing duets with him."[26] It appeared that he had found his true home at last.

Yet when Sidney Lanier made his first concert appearance in New York, it was not in one of Manhattan's great halls, or with any of New York's leading musical groups. Instead, he appeared at Association Hall in Brooklyn on 12 November 1873 in a benefit concert for the Sunday school of the Church of the Reformation. But Lanier's talents transcended the limits of notoriety usually imposed by such occasions; whereas this was "a concert of the sort not ordinarily noticed by newspapers, he played so successfully that the newspapers spoke of the concert as his debut."[27] Notices appeared in all the major journals of the city. The *Sun*, which called Lanier "a Southern gentleman who has become known as the author of a

----

[25]John Tasker Howard and George Kent Bellows, *A Short History of Music in America* (New York: Thomas Y. Crowell, 1957) 140-42.

[26]Starke, *Sidney Lanier*, 166.

[27]Ibid.

pleasant little romance of the late war," termed him "a flutist of remarkable skill and purity of style."[28] The Brooklyn *Eagle* spoke of him as "an admirable artist and thoroughly conversant with his instrument."[29] He played *Black-birds*, a nocturne by Briccialdi, and "in reply to an *encore* played Richardson's brilliant variations on 'The Blue Bells of Scotland.' "[30] The *New York Times* also noted Lanier's "debut" as the "most interesting incident" of the concert, and called *Black-birds* a "poetic fantasie upon the strain of the Southern blackbird, which it transforms into wild, sweet music, and, as a composition it is of classic purity, and decided originality."[31]

Alice G. Fletcher, known as a scholar of American Indian music, sent Lanier a fervent letter: "Your flute gave me that for which I had ceased to hope, true American Music. . . . when my soul hungered and thirsted for the Divine inspiration of music, I had to turn away to other lands and worship as it were in a foreign language. But when your music came . . . I found worship in my native land and tongue."[32]

Although pleased with all the ado, Lanier did not quite share the critics' exalted views. To him, the little concert was only a rehearsal for what he saw to be his real musical career in New York:

> I have had some pleasant musical successes. I played on Wednesday night at a concert in Brooklyn, before some 800 people, and made some stir, particularly in the papers. . . . Of course, the talk in the notices about a *debut*, the *debutant*, &c. is simply absurd: 'twas no *debut* at all, I only played for the fun of it and by way of feeling the pulse of the audiences in a quiet way . . . before venturing to prescribe for the big music-sick patient of New York. When I am ready to come out, which will be after I practice four months in Baltimore—I shall make my debut under the auspices of the

---

[28]New York *Sun*, 13 November 1873, Charles D. Lanier Collection, John Work Garrett Library, the Johns Hopkins University, Baltimore, Maryland.

[29]"Church of the Reformation Concert," Brooklyn *Eagle*, 13 November 1873, Charles D. Lanier Collection.

[30]New York *Evening Mail*, 13 November 1873, Charles D. Lanier Collection.

[31]"Music in Brooklyn," *New York Times*, 13 November 1873, Charles D. Lanier Collection.

[32]Alice G. Fletcher, "To Sidney Lanier," 14 November 1873, Charles D. Lanier Collection.

Philharmonic, or of Theo. Thomas,—or not at all. . . . There are so many
aspiring musicians here, who work for years and years, and are never heard
of at all.[33]

Lanier fulfilled his own prophecy. He never did, according to existing
records, make a formal debut with a major New York orchestra, although
he did play another recital, this time at the Church of the Holy Sepulchre
on 74th Street in Manhattan. Here he played Briccialdi's *Concertino, The
Blue Bells of Scotland,* and performed his own *Swamp Robin* as "a curious
psychologic study,—to note how it puzzled most of the audience."[34] Starke
speculates on what Theodore Thomas, "an appreciative critic of modern
music, thought of these pieces that invariably puzzled no matter how much
they delighted the audiences."[35] But there is also no evidence that Lanier
ever met Thomas or used the letter of introduction given him by Hamerik.
Lanier did meet Carl Wehner, Thomas's first flutist, and took some lessons with him. But Wehner, upon hearing Lanier's amazing virtuoso performance on his "8-keyed flute" exclaimed: "Here, give me that old thing
and take this Boehm. Aside from correcting some errors, there is nothing
I can teach you."

Although he enjoyed popularity and success in New York, Lanier never
accomplished his original, ambitious goals. On 19 November, Asger
Hamerik appeared in the city, asking Lanier to return to Baltimore for the
beginning of the Peabody orchestra season. The salary originally offered
had been halved by financial difficulties at the institute, but Lanier, having "had his little fling at the people of Babylon," decided to go to Baltimore.

The return to Baltimore was crucial in Lanier's development as a musician, for he was now earning his living with his flute, playing regularly
with professionals, and being exposed constantly to new and exciting music. It also marked the period during which his great poetry was to be written.

---

[33]Lanier, "To Mary Day Lanier," 16 November 1873, CE, 8:417.

[34]Lanier, "To Mary Day Lanier," 17 November 1873, ibid., 419.

[35]Starke, *Sidney Lanier,* 167.

CHAPTER III

Baltimore:
"The Monumental City"

LANIER RETURNED TO BALTIMORE in December 1873, and his immediate and warm reception into the city's professional circles is an indication of his genuinely superior indigenous talent. Here was a man with virtually no professional training, whose only experience in performing was limited to genteel musicales in small Southern cities, concerts with German groups in Texas, and two church recitals in New York. He also was unfamiliar with much of the standard symphonic repertory. Yet his immediate achievement of a place of prominence among internationally trained musicians denotes no lack of judgment on their part. Reviews always praised his playing, audiences loved him, and he was "speedily in demand as a soloist at all the musical organizations in the city," including the Germania Männerchor, the Liederkranz, and the festival choir of St. Paul's church.[1]

In addition to his friendships with Hamerik and Wysham, Lanier shared great respect and admiration with German-born pianist Nanette Falk-Auerbach, who, with Hamerik and Lanier, was the only member of the Baltimore group of that day to receive an entry in *Grove's Dictionary of Music and Musicians*. In a sonnet to her, Lanier declares her Beethoven's spiritual daughter.[2]

---

[1]Isabel L. Dobbin, "Lanier at the Peabody," *Peabody Bulletin* (April-May 1911): 4.

While Hamerik and others in Baltimore may have been affected by Lanier's magnetic charm, it is not likely that they would have accepted it as a substitute for ability. No idealistic and dedicated conductor bent on shaping a major conservatory and orchestra would allow less than major talent to work with him.

Baltimore had long displayed a love for music, entertaining scores of visiting performers from Europe and dozens of local groups. Here the sizable German community made an important contribution to the cultural life of the city; the Liederkranz, the most outstanding of the early local German organizations, did much to popularize Beethoven. But Baltimore did not become a national center of culture, taking its place with Boston, New York, and Philadelphia, until after the Civil War.

The city's cultural ascendance can be dated from 7 October 1866, when the Peabody Institute, endowed by successful merchant George Peabody, opened its doors. The institute's library and musical conservatory became major focal points of the intellectual and aesthetic life of the city. Under the innovative leadership of its second director, Asger Hamerik (who assumed this post in 1870), the orchestra became an organization of extremely high professional standards and commanded professional respect. The second institution whose establishment was to launch Baltimore into national prominence was the Johns Hopkins University, founded in 1876. And between these two giants Baltimore hosted dozens of smaller, but no less spirited, cultural organizations.

Four major German choral groups—the Liederkranz, Germania Männerchor, Harmonic, and Arion—presented concerts and "Sängerfeste" throughout the year.[3] A local musician, J. H. Rosewald, led performances of light opera. In the 1870s an opera house and the Academy of Music

[2]Sidney Lanier, "To Nanette Falk-Auerbach," in *The Centennial Edition of the Works of Sidney Lanier*, ed. Charles R. Anderson et al., 10 vols. (Baltimore: Johns Hopkins Press, 1945) 1:117 (hereafter cited as CE). It is said of Mme. Falk-Auerbach that she had "instant command" of all the Beethoven piano sonatas as well as the entire *Well-Tempered Clavier* of Bach (Waldo Selden Pratt, ed., *Grove's Dictionary of Music and Musicians, American Supplement* [Philadelphia: Theodore Presser, 1927] 119).

[3]Otto Ortmann, "Musical Baltimore in the Seventies," Baltimore *Evening Sun*, 16 July 1935.

were built, joining Concordia Hall, with seating for eighteen hundred, Lehmann's Hall, the Masonic Temple, the Germania Männerchor Hall, and the Monumental Assembly Rooms to offer all manner of entertainments from popular musicales to minstrel shows and melodramas.

Events at these halls were always posted on the front page of the Baltimore *Sun*. A typical day's offering featured "the eminent eccentric comedian," Mrs. James H. Stoddart, at Ford's Grand Opera House in Boucicault's *The Long Strike*, the "Thrilling Sensational Drama" *Skid*, a Grand Panorama of the Pacific Railroad, and a Great Troupe of Performing Dogs.[4] Another day's billing advertised the Peabody Orchestra, "The Great Moral Play of Uncle Tom's Cabin," a "Great Variety and Dramatic Show" at the New Central Theatre, and the "Singin' Skewl" at the Academy of Music.[5]

The atmosphere of musical life in Baltimore in the 1870s was one of fellowship, enthusiasm, and *Gemütlichkeit*. Informal musical soirees were held, the most notable at Otto Sutro's music store on West Baltimore Street. Clubs such as the Rossini Musical Association, the Haydn Musical Association, Baltimore Glee Club, Philharmonic Chorus, and Mendelssohn Octette flourished.[6]

However, for first-rank professional musicians, Baltimore was not home. Theodore Thomas's orchestra, the country's most prestigious ensemble, visited annually, as did numerous luminaries including Swedish diva Christine Nilsson, Russian pianist and composer Anton Rubinstein, Sir Arthur Sullivan, and even Franz Liszt. Whereas its musical life was exciting, Baltimore could not be truly vital until it produced its own standard of professionalism, with an orchestra that could rival that of Thomas.

Asger Hamerik was brought to Baltimore to provide this vitality. Born in Denmark in 1843, Hamerik had studied with Hans von Bülow and was an intimate of Edvard Grieg and Hector Berlioz. He enjoyed a solid reputation in Europe as a composer when he accepted the Peabody's offer. Encouraged by his colleagues' confidence in America's growing appetite for music, by the warm receptions accorded Europeans in Baltimore, and

---

[4]Baltimore *Sun*, 8 December 1873, 1.

[5]Ibid., 6 April 1878, 1.

[6]Ortmann, "Musical Baltimore."

by "reports of the sixteen thousand-odd folios at the Peabody," Hamerik undertook the responsibilities of his new position, eagerly optimistic. He was a "non-conformist incarnate,"[7] now presented with an opportunity to test new ideas and new music.

Hamerik faced considerable obstacles in Baltimore. He had to contend with a German-dominated musical community and audiences whose palates were accustomed to German tastes; Hamerik wanted to introduce them to Scandinavian and "futuristic" music. His board of directors did not always agree with his methods—Hamerik sought to educate, not merely entertain, and refused to pander to his audiences' appetites—which put him in a defensive position when box-office receipts were not enough to offset the orchestra's expenses. Even fairly successful subscription drives proved to be "little more than a stop-gap measure in the face of the rising costs of concerts and the Institute's shrinking endowment. The high artistic standards maintained by Hamerik, especially his own personal unbending zeal to program contemporary music, virtually eliminated any possibility of broad support from the community and contributed to the eventual abandonment of the symphony concerts."[8]

Yet Hamerik was liked personally and was warmly welcomed into the community. He infused the Peabody with a new spirit enjoyed by his fellow artists. His concert series, student concerts, and afternoon faculty recitals made the conservatory on Mount Vernon Place a focal point of the city's cultural activity. Aesthetically, Hamerik was a godsend for the Peabody, for, under his direction, it changed Baltimore from a laggard to a leader; low box-office returns seem to have been a small price for creating a national reputation for the conservatory. The first decade of Hamerik's tenure—the years when Lanier was a member of the orchestra—appears to have been a dynamic and adventurous era. During this time academic standards were raised; the conservatory was visited and praised by Rubinstein, von Bülow, and Sullivan; the orchestra presented the Baltimore

[7]Lubov Keefer, *Baltimore's Music: The Haven of the American Composer* (Baltimore: J. H. Furst, 1962) 178.

[8]Ray Edward Robinson, *The Peabody Conservatory: An American Solution to a European Musical Philosophy*, 2 vols. (Baltimore: Peabody Conservatory, 1963) 1:230.

premieres of many important works; and, in 1877, the first American Beethoven Memorial Festival was held here.[9]

Not allowing himself to be deterred by the poor financial condition of the orchestra, Hamerik persevered in his desire to bring new and challenging music to Baltimore. The following works—most of which were contemporary, even avant-garde, since many of the composers were still active—were first introduced to Baltimore by Hamerik: Beethoven's *Choral Fantasy* and *Symphony #9*, Berlioz's *Symphonie Fantastique*, Brahms's *Symphony #1*, Chopin's *Concerto in E Minor* for piano, Dvorak's *Slavonic Rhapsody*, Neils Gade's *Third Symphony*, the *Ocean Symphony* of Rubinstein, Saint-Säens's *Concerto in G Minor* and *Symphony in A Minor*, Tchaikovsky's *Symphony #6* ("Pathetique"), and the Overture to *Tannhäuser* by Wagner.[10] Many of Hamerik's own works appeared frequently in the Peabody's concert programs, and for the most part, his works—many of which were programmatic in nature, such as the *Norse Suites* and the *Jewish Trilogy*—were well received by audiences.

Hamerik was also an advocate of original American music, regarding it as a school and deserving of a place beside those of Germany and Scandinavia. His concerts were often presented thematically; that is, they would be devoted entirely to the music of a specific period or country. Theodore Thomas's orchestra also presented thematically organized concerts; nights devoted to particular composers (such as Mendelssohn, Beethoven, or Mozart) appear in his New York City Garden concert repertoire as early as 1866. But "national" concerts, such as those devoted to Scandinavian and English music, do not appear until the summer of 1874,[11] suggesting that Thomas may have been influenced by the programming of conservatories. However, Thomas wrote in 1904: "I have never wished to pose as an educator. . . . Nor has it been a fad of mine, as some people have imagined, to persevere for half a century and insist upon preserving the unity of a programme."[12]

---

[9]Ibid., 2:3; 1877 was the fiftieth anniversary of Beethoven's death.

[10]Ibid., 1:231.

[11]Theodore Thomas, *A Musical Autobiography*, ed. George P. Upton, 2 vols. (Chicago: A. C. McClurg, 1905) 2:n.p.

[12]Ibid., introduction, 2:17.

Hamerik's programs were designed to educate, to give opportunities to contemporary composers, and to give audiences an appreciation of style and national flavor. There were "Italian School" evenings, German nights, and American nights featuring the works of such contemporary composers as George Bristow (b. 1825), Otis B. Boise (b. 1844), Alfred H. Pease (b. 1838), and William K. Bassford (b. 1839).[13] These American concerts initially met negative criticism, and Hamerik had to defend his philosophy to the trustees. In his 1874 report to the provost and trustees, he wrote:

> In establishing an academy of music in America rather than elsewhere, there was evidently an intention on Mr. Peabody's part to give some opportunity not only for American performers, but also for native composers, and whatever might be of value in American music. Recognizing the fact that there are very decided differences in the schools of music in the different countries, I endeavored to make the concerts of the past season systematic and characteristic, and so arranged them as to exemplify the peculiarities of the different schools. The American concert was, perhaps, less successful than the others, mainly because of the newness of the music, and so requiring a larger number of rehearsals than could conveniently be given.[14]

But Hamerik persisted in his own style of programming and was rewarded the next year when his "American Night" received encouraging notice. "There has been neither as enthusiastic a concert," wrote the *Sun*, "nor as well filled a house during this season as at the Peabody Conservatory on Saturday night. Mr. Hamerik doubtless offered the best that our limited American repertory could afford, and the performers unquestionably made the best of the works he selected. . . . The concert, taken altogether, was a great success, and gives hope that the day is not far distant when we may boast of a national school of composers."[15]

---

[13]Peabody Orchestra concert program, 13 March 1875, Charles D. Lanier Collection, John Work Garrett Library, the Johns Hopkins University, Baltimore, Maryland.

[14]*Seventh Annual Report of the Provost to the Trustees* (Baltimore: Peabody Institute, 4 June 1874).

[15]"Eleventh Peabody Concert—American Night," Baltimore *Sun*, 15 March 1875.

By 1873, the atmosphere that Hamerik had established at the Peabody was the best that Lanier could have hoped for; it suited him ideally. Not only was he in a city steeped in the German culture he loved so well, but he was also aligned with a young conductor open to innovation, who encouraged other composers, and who was himself an advocate of the union of poetry and music.

This was the circle into which Lanier was drawn. From his first meeting with Hamerik, he found himself warmly gathered into Baltimore's musical society, and for the first time his talents were recognized on a professional level. In the years to follow, he would be tendered invitations by every major organization in the city: the Baltimore Glee Club, the Club Germania, the Maryland Academy of Sciences, the Musical Union of Baltimore, the Allston Association, and the Maryland Historical Society.[16] On 2 February 1876, he was elected a member (with Hamerik, music critic Innes Randolph, and several members of the Peabody faculty) of the famous Wednesday Club.[17] Aubrey Starke places emphasis on the significance of Lanier belonging "to the Musical Section rather than to the Literary Section" of the Wednesday Club."[18]

---

[16]Invitations, membership cards, and passes issued to Lanier are in the Henry W. Lanier Collection, Milton S. Eisenhower Library, the Johns Hopkins University, Baltimore, Maryland.

[17]"Book of Records of the Wednesday Club 1869-86." The minutes of the meeting of 2 February 1876 (p. 49) record Lanier's name in the list of new members. Maryland Historical Society, Baltimore.

[18]Aubrey Harrison Starke, "Sidney Lanier as a Musician," *Musical Quarterly* 20 (October 1934): 396.

CHAPTER IV

The Influence
of the Related Arts Movement

THE MOST IMPORTANT RESULT of Lanier's trip to New York was his exposure to the new music arriving from Europe and to an abundance of new American music. In both of these areas, the works most influential upon him belong to the genre of composition that began to flourish in the nineteenth century: programme music. The development of this type of music—transcription in sound of intellectual concepts—was a major contribution of the Romantic era. An exploration of the idea of programme music will show why it appealed to Lanier and how it influenced his own creativity.

Programme music is the opposite of absolute music, which relies purely upon musical tone and structure to create an impression upon the listener. It involves more than music—it is inspired by things external to it, perhaps a natural scene, a painting, an event, or a poem. The idea of combining two or more arts to create a unified artistic expression was characteristic of the Romantic age, resulting in musical poetry and poetic music.[1] An interest in using one sense expression to evoke another sensual impression—synaesthesia—was especially prominent in Germany, where philosophers and artists dreamed of "color-hearing," "tone-painting," "statues that could become paintings," and "paintings that would be

---

[1]Hugo Leichentritt, *Music, History, and Ideas* (Cambridge: Harvard University Press, 1938) 209.

poems."[2] But the most widespread manifestation of synaesthesia was that of programme music.

The concept was not new to the nineteenth century, as at least one contemporary critic was quick to point out; in an 1875 article in *Dwight's Journal of Music* (the country's most influential music periodical, published in Boston), G. A. Macfarren cites works of Buxtehude, Bach, Vivaldi, and Handel as precursors of compositions written during the current interest in pieces "purposing to paint in tones the pictures announced in the titles they choose."[3] Corelli's *Christmas Concerto*, Vivaldi's *Four Seasons*, and the "Pastoral Symphony" from Handel's *Messiah* are all early examples of translating nonmusical ideas into tone. But the Romantic spirit of the nineteenth century created a whole new flowering of multimediate expressions. The dominant composers of nineteenth-century programme music were German—Mendelssohn, Schubert, Beethoven, Liszt, Wagner—as Germany was the world's musical voice of authority. The titanic Berlioz, with his increasingly popular *Symphonie Fantastique*, was France's leader in the genre. By the end of the century, the nationalist movement in composition, a development of programme music fired by patriotism, was flourishing; composers such as Smetana, Dvorak, Tchaikovsky, Grieg, and Raff were all embodying within their music the landscapes, history, and folk-life of their countries.

Music of great European composers was already familiar to Americans long before the Civil War. A Handel and Haydn Society had been founded in Boston in 1815, and five years later the Musical Fund Society was established. Other cities subsequently organized music clubs, and by mid-century, classical and romantic music was known in most large American cities.[4] The visits of famous European performers, such as the virtuoso violinist Ole Bull and Jenny Lind, "the Swedish Nightingale," further popularized European music. The Germania Society arrived from Germany in 1848 and was the first successful orchestra to tour all the important cities

---

[2]Charmenz S. Lenhart, *Musical Influence on American Poetry* (Athens: University of Georgia Press, 1956) 84.

[3]"The Pictorial Power of Music," *Dwight's Journal of Music* (24 July 1875): 1.

[4]Carl Bode, *Antebellum Culture* (Carbondale: Southern Illinois University Press, 1970) 30.

of America; Carl Zerrahn, its flute player, settled in Boston and founded an orchestra that was a predecessor of the Boston Symphony.[5]

After the Civil War, however, new European music arrived in Boston, New York, and Philadelphia. By this time professional musicianship in America had developed to the point where this music could be performed competently. Two groups that introduced and popularized much of this music were the New York orchestras of Theodore Thomas and Leopold Damrosch. Thomas was especially fervent in his advocacy of programme music, which led to an occasional confrontation. American audiences, more interested in novelty than aesthetics, were often rude and unreceptive, and this Thomas would not tolerate. On one occasion in New York, the audience was annoyed at Thomas's insistence upon performing new and complex works and noisily disturbed the playing of Liszt's *Mephisto Waltz*. Thomas angrily declared that he would wait five minutes for any objectors to leave the concert hall and then proceed with the program despite the opinion of the audience. There was silence immediately, and the concert continued.[6]

Program notes to Thomas's concerts demonstrate his devotion to descriptive music. A typical program is the one for 20 December 1873, when the Philharmonic Society of Brooklyn, conducted by Thomas, performed at the Academy of Music; the works presented were *Symphony #3* ("In the Forest") by Joseph Joachim Raff, Berlioz's *Queen Mab Scherzo*, and the *Hungarian Rhapsody #2* of Liszt. The program notes state that Raff's symphony "belongs to the descriptive school of music, and is evidently modelled after the Pastoral Symphony of Beethoven." The notes on Liszt are more didactic:

> The change in feeling, not only in this country, but in Europe, in respect to the Liszt-Wagner School of Music will be observed by those at all familiar with the progress of musical taste in the new and old world. . . . The adherents of the new school in this country are exceedingly numerous. Indeed a programme is regarded as scarcely complete unless either Liszt or Wagner is represented. Whatever may be said to their capacity to touch

---

[5]John Tasker Howard and George Kent Bellows, *A Short History of Music in America* (New York: Thomas Y. Crowell, 1957) 114.

[6]David Ewen, *Music Comes to America* (New York: Thomas Y. Crowell, 1942) 31-32.

the popular heart, there can be no doubt of their excellent influence upon other composers who have been compelled to put more brains into their work. The cultivated taste is no longer content with meaningless melody. It demands ideas.[7]

Sidney Lanier did not attend this concert; he was in Baltimore at the time. But this program is among his papers, perhaps sent by a New York friend. These ideas reflect his own, though, for he was fascinated by the "orchestral interpretation" of "intellectual conceptions" and all of his own work in musical composition is based upon "ideas."

Asger Hamerik was also ardent in his support of programme music. His concert programs reflect his concern with the phenomenon of descriptive music, and a glance through the selections played during Lanier's tenure reveals a wide range of compositions that must have impressed and inspired the poet's conceptions. Concerts during the eighth season (1874-1875) featured Berlioz's *Symphonie Fantastique* (played frequently over the years) and Niels W. Gade's *Norse Symphony*,[8] with notes to both works provided. Other programmatic works featured by Hamerik were Berlioz's *Symphonic Poem on "King Lear"* and the Prelude to Act Four of the opera *Tovelille*, with "poetry and music by Asger Hamerik."

Subsequent concert seasons were highlighted by such programmatic pieces as von Bülow's *The Minstrel's Curse*, Hamerik's *Jewish Trilogy*, the *William Tell* overture by Rossini, Emil Hartmann's *Raid of the Vikings*, and Mikhail Glinka's *Kamarinskaya*.[9] Lanier's letters attest to the great excitement he felt upon first hearing some of this new music: "O my Heart, O my Twin, if thou cdst. but be by me in this sublime glory of music! . . . The beauty of it maketh me catch my breath,—to write it. I will not at-

---

[7]Program of 20 December 1873, Charles D. Lanier Collection, John Work Garrett Library, the Johns Hopkins University, Baltimore, Maryland.

[8]An early critic of Gade (1817-1890) notes that the composer was also a devotee of the related arts: "To form a true idea of the man, it will be well to remember his love of the . . . sister arts of music, painting and sculpture. . . . The motto of his Op. 1 shows in what spirit Gade entered upon his career: 'Formulas hold us not, our art's name is poesy.' " Frederick Niecks, *Programme Music in the Last Four Centuries* (London: Novello, 1907) 396.

[9]Concert programs, Charles D. Lanier Collection, John Work Garrett Library.

tempt to describe it. It is the Spirit of the Poems of Ossian, done in music by the wonderful Niels Gade."[10]

Lanier was also sensitive to the vivid suggestions these works offered his own art. Doubtless, too, Lanier was affected by the emphasis placed upon the related arts by contemporary journals. Although he probably could not afford to subscribe to *Dwight's Journal of Music* (nor did the Peabody have it in its library), he was sure to find it circulated among his friends and read therein such articles as "The Pictorial Power of Music" and "Poets and Composers of Music," which suggests that "the musician should be an elocutionist in the language of words as well as in that of music."[11] He might also have read an article in the 2 May 1874 *Dwight's Journal* entitled "The Poetic Basis of Music" by Joseph Bennett, reprinted from the *London Musical Times*. Attempting to explain Wagner's "underlying principles," Bennett quotes from a recently published book by Franz Hüffer, *The Music of the Future*. Beethoven's *Symphony #3*, says Hüffer, is "the foundation of the great development of modern German, and especially of Wagner's own, music. The principle of this new phase in art . . . *is the necessity of a poetical basis of music.*" However, Bennett disagrees with the entire theory, suggesting that Wagner, "having a mission" and "being at the head of a movement, would make the little sphere in which he works comprise the whole world."[12] Lanier, as a Wagnerophile, would have sided with Hüffer against Bennett.

Appleton's Journal of Literature, Science, and Art, to which Lanier also had access, carried articles on all subjects, including music, drama, and poetry. Mary Day Lanier apparently read it and, imbued with her husband's ideals as deeply as he, was moved to make the following suggestion to him in February 1874: "If thou hast not already seen it, read in Apple-

---

[10]Sidney Lanier, "To Mary Day Lanier," 2 December 1873, in *The Centennial Edition of the Works of Sidney Lanier*, ed. Charles R. Anderson et al., 10 vols. (Baltimore: Johns Hopkins Press, 1945) 8:424-26 (hereafter cited as CE); also Lanier, "To Mary Day Lanier," 11 December 1873, ibid., 429; Lanier, "To Mary Day Lanier," 21 December 1873, ibid., 437-38; Lanier, "To Mary Day Lanier," 3 January 1874, CE, 9:4.

[11]*Dwight's Journal of Music* (25 May 1878): 233-34.

[12]Joseph Bennett, "The Poetic Basis of Music," *Dwight's Journal of Music* (2 May 1874): 219.

ton's of Jan. 17th—Page 92.—the article under the heading of 'Music'. 'Tis a good, comprehensive setting-forth of the Symphony Orchestra, and must have been written by a good musician or musical critic. Do not fail to read it."[13] This article bemoans the lack of American institutions of conservatory quality—music schools that would offer instruction and performance opportunities. "This crowning agency in a musical curriculum is absent in America from all our so-called conservatories, except from the Peabody Institute in Baltimore. . . . [It is] the only school in the United States which embodies the leading features of a great musical school."[14] The author goes on to praise the Peabody's curriculum, concert series, and director.

One particular article published in the spring of 1874 definitely should have attracted Lanier's notice, for it seems almost deliberately addressed to him:

> If the theory of the music of the future be a correct one—that is, that the excellence of music is in the ratio of its significance as the embodiment of thought and feeling, and not for the sole sake of sonorous beauty—then, according to the *Examiner*, "it follows that the musician of the future must be a poet; that, however richly gifted with a natural feeling for melody, or skilled in the technicalities of musical art, these endowments and accomplishments will go for nothing unless he can compose a poetical text."[15]

Looming above all other exponents of a related-arts theory was Richard Wagner, and his growing sphere of influence included Lanier. Apparently having read Wagner's prose before hearing his work in one of Thomas's New York concerts in the summer of 1870, he had written to Mary, "The 'Music of the Future' is surely thy music and my music."[16] He was referring to Wagner's *Das Kunstwerk der Zukunft*, a critical work written in 1850, which outlines the composer's theory of an art form that unites

---

[13]Mary Day Lanier to Sidney Lanier, 5 February 1874, Charles D. Lanier Collection, Milton S. Eisenhower Library, the Johns Hopkins University, Baltimore, Maryland.

[14]*Appleton's Journal of Literature, Science, and Art* (17 January 1874): 92.

[15]*Appleton's Journal* (21 March 1874): 381-82.

[16]Lanier, "To Mary Day Lanier," 15 August 1870, CE, 8:99.

all the separate arts.[17] Although Wagner is considered primarily a composer, he himself considered poetry the superior art; he asserted that "melodic verse itself must be the 'life-giving center' of the dramatic structure."[18] Wagner is also characterized by his "musical pictorializations," in which the shape of the musical line reflects the meaning of the lyrics (for example, an ascending line depicting a character's upward physical motion); although this is not Wagner's original idea, this technique is so central to his works that it has become very closely associated with him.

How much of *Das Kunstwerk der Zukunft* Lanier actually read, and how closely, is a matter of speculation, but over the years he drew increasing inspiration from the German master and was able to appraise Wagner's music intelligently and sympathetically while it was still beset with controversy.[19] Lanier could identify with Wagner in many ways: they both believed in a synthesis of the arts; both had creative talents in more than one field (Wagner wrote all of his opera libretti as well as many works of criticism); and both were met with resistance by the artistic establishments of their day. When, in the 1850s, Carl Bergmann, an early conductor of the New York Philharmonic, introduced the overture to *Tannhäuser*, the *New York Times* reviewer assailed Wagner, and Bergmann suffered a great loss of popularity because of his advocacy of Wagner and Liszt, who were "generally disliked." But Bergmann's obstinacy ultimately triumphed, at least in musical terms; by 1876, the year of Bergmann's death, Wagner and Liszt were warmly received by New York concert audiences,[20] and Wagner had been asked to compose a march for the festivities marking the American centennial.

Lanier also felt an ideological tie to Wagner. As a result of his bent to align music with morality, Lanier admired Wagner's disdain of "Trade" and idolized him as an embodiment of the creator of social betterment through music. In Lanier's "To Richard Wagner" (1877), the superior

---

[17]Jack M. Stein, *Richard Wagner and the Synthesis of the Arts* (Detroit: Wayne State University Press, 1960) 63.

[18]Ibid., 49.

[19]Aubrey Harrison Starke, *Sidney Lanier: A Biographical and Critical Study* (reprint, New York: Russell and Russell, 1964) 288.

[20]Ewen, *Music Comes to America*, 38-39.

forces of music and faith overcome the darkness of "murk and factories."
Wagner, as a composer of "big ballads of the modern heart," had the "power
to say the Time in terms of tone." Lanier saw Wagner as the "musical
prophet of a new age, an age of industry, more noble than an age of Trade,
in which work should be performed to the sublime strains of divine music.
. . . in *Tannhäuser* especially, with its theme of the life-long antagonism
of good and evil, he found an opera dear to his soul, the work of a brother
artist."[21] Fired by this admiration, Lanier planned to translate Wagner's
libretti for the *Ring* cycle, but apparently only got as far as forty lines of
Das Rheingold.[22]

The other German composer whose works were featured by both
Thomas and Hamerik was Franz Liszt, famous as an idolized piano virtuoso
and, as a composer, the originator of the "symphonic poem." This was
Liszt's term for "large-scale orchestral compositions which are not in any
one of the generally recognized musical forms, and which follow or illustrate a prescribed programme."[23] Calvin S. Brown writes that the original
idea of the symphonic poem seems to have been, to Liszt, the transposi-
tion of specific poems into music; many of the symphonic poems are based
upon works by Byron, Schiller, Lamartine, and Hugo.[24] In his writings,
Lanier indicates his familiarity with several compositions by Liszt, including his "translation into music of Lamartine's Meditation upon Death"[25]
and the "tone-poem of Immortality."[26]

---

[21]Starke, *Sidney Lanier*, 288. Jack DeBellis notes that "Good moral feeling
could actually be demonstrated through Wagner's music, though Lanier would
have been shocked had he taken a more careful look at the moral implications of
the 'Ring' cycle." Jack DeBellis, *Sidney Lanier* (New York: Twayne, 1972) 70-71.
Lanier probably would have been further disillusioned to learn of Wagner's big-
otry and social behavior.

[22]CE, 9:112 n.132.

[23]Robert Illing, A *Dictionary of Music* (Baltimore: Penguin, 1950) 269.

[24]Calvin S. Brown, *Music and Literature: A Comparison of the Arts* (Athens:
University of Georgia Press, 1948) 224.

[25]"The Centennial Cantata," CE, 2:270.

[26]"From Bacon to Beethoven," ibid., 279.

A third composer of programme music whose name appears repeatedly in the Peabody concert records is Hector Berlioz, Hamerik's teacher. Berlioz's major composition, *Symphonie Fantastique*, seems to have been one of the orchestra's most popular works in the repertory.

Lanier's ardent advocacy of programme music was expressed three ways: he played it enthusiastically; he wrote it; and he wrote about it. In his 1876 essay "From Bacon to Beethoven," he discusses the style as a controversial but ultimately satisfying form:

> For example, there are many conscientious and beautiful-souled artists who deny themselves all the glory and delight to be found in the so-called "programme-music." Their motives are unquestionably those of rigourous conscientiousness. Programme-music has been held up to them as a sort of unclean thing. It is indeed no wonder at all that the steady-going classicists should have been startled and alarmed by the tremendous explosion of Berlioz in their midst. At this distance of time, the quiet thinker who has not been brought up in the traditions of any school can easily see that in the state of music at that period a clap of good rousing thunder was exactly the best thing which could happen, and for this purpose Berlioz was sent.[27]

Not everyone was as thrilled with the new music as were Lanier and Hamerik. The Baltimore correspondent for *Dwight's Journal,* who signed himself "Musikus," found several occasions on which to disparage the Peabody's concert fare. His report on the 1875 season notes that "The new composers seem to have the lion's share in it,—naturally enough, since the conductor, Prof. Asger Hamerik, is one of them."[28] In February 1879, Musikus writes that the thirty-two-member orchestra is "scarcely able to cope with the new music of the new schools, for which our ambitious director entertains so dedicated a predilection. . . . the opinion of your correspondent is that we can well afford to do without the clashing innovations of Berlioz and Saint-Saëns for a season."[29] Two months later he repeats that "pure old classical music" is preferable to the audience rather than "labored interpretation of the music of the new school. . . . Our general

[27]Ibid., 278-79.

[28]*Dwight's Journal of Music* (24 July 1875): 136.

[29]Ibid., (1 February 1879): 16.

audiences are not ready for the music of the future, and it is very doubtful
when they will be. What they need now is the good old music of the past."[30]

If Musikus accurately reported the reactions of Baltimore, the ultimate
collapse of the subscription concerts at the Peabody is understandable, since
the avant-garde is never immediately popular with general audiences. But
as far as Lanier's development is concerned, anything less than Hamerik's
courageous programming would have had a stultifying effect. He, unlike
Musikus, was a poet.

---

[30]Ibid., (12 April 1879): 56.

CHAPTER V

American Music
and the Music of Lanier

THE CONSTANT INFLUENCE of programme music was only one of the forces that directed Lanier toward his own creative efforts. A second was the rising clamor for genuine American music, and with it the encouragement of American composers. Whereas there had not been a lack of American composers, they had always worked with European materials. Gilbert Chase notes that our early popular and folk music were derived from European music, but "became gradually transformed" by the American experience; yet no such process took place with art music, which stayed essentially European for generations.[1]

Initially, American music was based upon English, then Italian models, as the music of Italian composers gained popularity in this country in the 1830s. Even composers who seriously attacked the problem of creating "American" music encountered difficulties. One of these was Anthony Philip Heinrich, born in Bohemia in 1781. Having emigrated to America in 1810, he attempted to convey in music his impressions of places visited in the United States and became a champion of native American music. Yet when he brought out his first collection of compositions, *The Dawning of Music in Kentucky, or the Pleasures of Harmony in the Solitudes of Nature* (1820), it was promptly compared with European music, and Heinrich was

---

[1]Gilbert Chase, *America's Music: From the Pilgrims to the Present*, rev. 2d ed. (New York: McGraw-Hill, 1966) 325.

dubbed "The Beethoven of America."[2] It may have been American in Heinrich's mind, but it was Germanic to the ear, sounding as if it were composed by a European disciple of Beethoven. America's first two operas, William Henry Fry's *Leonora* (1845) and George Frederick Bristow's *Rip Van Winkle* (1855), were both imitative of the Italian operatic mode, even though the latter work was based upon American literature.[3] By the 1860s, when Germany was the acknowledged world leader in artistic matters, American music sounded German. Because the models for fine-art music were imported, writes Chase, "they failed to provide the American composer with 'a usable past,' and operative tradition."[4]

As with the continuing debate about literature, the question of what made music "American" was long-standing and controversial. If it was defined as "music composed in this country"—a phrase used in the constitution of the New York Philharmonic Society—it could be interpreted to mean music written by visiting musicians or those who had emigrated to this country.[5] This was just the case with the Philharmonic, with the result that native composers were virtually ignored, a fact publicly protested by Bristow, himself a member of the orchestra, and by Fry, who in the winter of 1872-1873, delivered in New York a famous series of lectures on the arts. Here he cried out for a "Declaration of Independence in Art on the part of American composers. Let them cease to bow down to a Handel, a Mozart, or a Beethoven. Let them strike out into untrodden realms, guided only by nature and their own inspirations."[6] The result of all this agitation was that the Philharmonic did begin to grant more consideration to the native composer, but the composer himself still paid homage to Europe.

With the founding of the great conservatories in Germany—Leipzig in 1843, Berlin in 1850, and Dresden in 1855—Americans began a long

---

[2]John Tasker Howard and George Kent Bellows, *A Short History of Music in America* (New York: Thomas Y. Crowell, 1957) 124-25.

[3]Ibid., 128.

[4]Chase, *America's Music*, 325.

[5]Ibid., 327.

[6]Ibid., 332. Chase notes the irony of this plea coming from a man who wrote opera imitative of Bellini.

educational pilgrimage, and "very few [serious] American students found themselves in Florence or Paris."[7] With the immigration of thousands of Germans to the United States in the 1840s and 1850s, concert tours by European musicians, and the education of American artists under German masters, this country was thoroughly inundated by foreign musical influences. Two of America's most successful nineteenth-century composers, John Knowles Paine and Dudley Buck—who would later collaborate with Lanier—were both German-trained. Until the establishment of the first American conservatories in the 1860s, there could be no native school of music with respect to training.

However, in terms of native subject matter, American art-music was beginning to flourish,[8] with Buck and Paine leading the way. In addition to the *Centennial Meditation of Columbia*, which was composed to Lanier's words for the 1876 American Centennial Exhibition, Buck wrote a second cantata based upon American literature, *The Voyage of Columbus*, from Washington Irving's *Life of Columbus*. Paine, "our leading academic com-

---

[7]William Treat Upton, *Art-Song in America: A Study in the Development of American Music* (Boston: Oliver Ditson, 1930) 37-38.

[8]Two prominent composers, Stephen Foster and Louis Moreau Gottschalk, are not discussed here—Foster because he did not write art music (symphonies, concerti, chamber music), and Gottschalk because he was "isolated" from the center of American musical life by geography (he was born to Louisiana Creole society, education, and travel). Gottschalk did write a "folkloristic" type of programme music that was influenced by black, Caribbean, and Creole modes, and exemplified by such pieces as *The Banjo, Ojos Criollos, Grande Caprice on the Argentine National Anthem*, and *La Noche de los Trópicos* (Chase, *America's Music*, 309-20). Yet Gottschalk always remained "an exotic personality within his native country" (ibid., 302). Some of Gottschalk's pieces were popular as "salon" music in the United States, and Lanier developed an early affinity for his compositions. "Gottschalk is to me, a Miracle," he wrote in 1862. "His Music produces in me a supernatural thrill. . . . Beethoven is wild: but Gottschalk's wildness is more etherial [sic], more spirituelle. . . . His Music lifts me out of myself, until I almost lose consciousness of my own individuality" (Lanier, "To Augusta Lamar," May 1862[?] in *The Centennial Edition of the Works of Sidney Lanier*, ed. Charles R. Anderson et al., 10 vols. [Baltimore: Johns Hopkins Press, 1945] 7:59 [hereafter cited as CE]). Lanier's appraisal of Gottschalk's work, as with all his other youthful expression about music, was emotional. He never mentions Gottschalk after leaving the South.

poser,"[9] also wrote a piece for the 1876 exhibition, a setting of John Greenleaf Whittier's *Centennial Hymn*. For the 1893 Chicago World's Fair, he wrote the *Columbia March and Hymn*, and, for the St. Louis Exposition in 1904, he composed *Hymn of the West*. Frederick Grant Gleason, who studied with Buck and then went to Germany, wrote a cantata with orchestra based upon Joseph Rodman Drake's *The Culprit Fay*.[10]

The American conservatory was the logical place for the encouragement of American music, and the Peabody introduced its musicians and audiences to many native composers (all of whom are now, unfortunately, virtually forgotten). The concert of 25 January 1874 featured the *Symphony-Concerto in G minor* by Otis B. Boise, an air from Paine's oratorio *St. Peter*, and the *Wedding March* by J. H. Rosewald, who was concertmaster of the Peabody orchestra. "American Night" on 13 March 1875 presented the *Arcadian Symphony* of George Frederick Bristow, songs by Alfred H. Pease, the introduction to the opera *Cassilda* by William K. Bassford, and a repetition of Boise's *Concerto*.[11] Reviewers, even when critical of specific pieces, acclaimed the encouragement of native composers. Opinions on native music varied throughout the country, however, from that of the editor of *Dwight's Journal*, John S. Dwight, whose scorn of native efforts resulted from his absolute worship of all things Germanic, to the beliefs of those who felt, as Herman Melville did in regard to American literature, that even mediocre creations of native composers deserved praise before excellent foreign works.

What is important is that the atmosphere generated in musical circles, especially in the growing new conservatories, was encouraging to native talent; therefore, when Lanier began to compose more ambitious pieces, he found a receptive milieu. Hearing new music written by Americans who were his contemporaries was undoubtedly added incentive. The music that he wrote in Baltimore reflects the two major forces at work upon him: the encouragement of American music, especially under Hamerik's enthusiasm; and the emphasis upon related arts, which determined that all of his

---

[9]Chase, *America's Music*, 337.

[10]Ibid., 336-38.

[11]Original programs, Charles D. Lanier Papers, John Work Garrett Library, the Johns Hopkins University, Baltimore, Maryland.

music would be programmatic, and which also shaped his most powerful poetry.

What was Lanier's music like, and how does it fit into the context of American music that was being produced during his lifetime? His career as a composer can be said to epitomize America's creative musical effort: it began with imitation and matured into originality.

His earliest complete compositions—there are many undated fragments in his musical papers—are simple songs, just as his earliest poems are dominated by the song-concept.[12] These are graceful and sentimental parlor-piano art songs that seem to reflect the influence of German *lieder*,[13] and this view can be reinforced by noting that several of them were written during his German-dominated San Antonio days. The songs are not complicated; the vocal lines are lyrical and sometimes eloquent, but the piano accompaniments are usually little more than repetitive chordal patterns. But with his move to Baltimore and his exposure to more complex music, he began to conceive freer melodic lines and develop musical interaction, or dialogue, between flute and piano. It is significant to note that Lanier dated his career as a composer from the time he entered his professional life in Baltimore and contrasting his pre-Baltimore songs with his later compositions provides further proof of his aesthetic development.

Lanier's first song, *Little Ella*, is lovely to the ear, but its words (this is Lanier's only song for which he also wrote the lyrics) are sentimental and awkward:

> O, exquisite rare, O past compare
> Was that young star soul shining there,
> In an eye that gleamed dark-bright like dawn,
> When dews first sparkle on the lawn.[14]

The last line is a true disappointment, especially when it is remembered that the song is dedicated to a child who literally saved Lanier's life. It is a self-consciously constructed song; delicate runs and graceful notes, while

---

[12]Charmenz Lenhart points out the song-concept in Lanier's early poetry (*Musical Influence on American Poetry* [Athens: University of Georgia Press, 1956] 239).

[13]This was suggested to the author by soprano Florence Peacock.

[14]CE, 1:9.

creating a challenge to the singer, actually detract from the smoothness
of melodic line:

As an example of a nineteenth-century American sentimental song,
this is not very different from some of the works of the country's most popular songwriter, Stephen Foster. It is somewhat similar to an 1853 Foster
song entitled *Little Ella*,[16] which is also a melodic tribute to a child (a favorite subject of nineteenth-century American balladists), and includes a
listing of her attributes; she is "Like a brooklet running brightly / In the
genial smile of May, / Like a breeze upon the meadows / All besprent with
early flowers, / Like a bird mid sylvan shadows." Lanier's Ella is "As soft
as the passion of flowers for dew, / As wild as a wave when tempests woo,
/ As high as a lark's flight up the blue." The rising bird-flight is given an
ascending line in both songs:

(Lanier)

---

[15]Original manuscript, Charles D. Lanier Papers, John Work Garrett Library.

[16]Stephen Collins Foster, *Songs and Compositions*, produced by Walter R.
Whittlesey et al. (Indianapolis: Foster Hall Reproductions, 1933) case 2.

like a bird - - mid - - syl - - van shad - - ows
(Foster)

This does not mean that Lanier took from Foster the idea of writing a musical line to suit the meaning of the vocal line; this was a historically common compositional technique and can be noted, for instance, in the cantatas of Bach and the oratorios of Handel. It means that both Foster and Lanier utilized this common technique in their compositions, following a long-established pattern. Nor does this allege that Lanier's *Little Ella* is plagiarism. It may have been inspired in part by Foster's song—or by any of the hundreds of contemporary sentimental songs about children—but there is no evidence to indicate that Lanier ever even heard it. What is indicated is that at this point in his musical career, Lanier was not composing creatively; he was merely falling into a tradition and following the current, conventional modes. But the positive aspect of *Little Ella* is that it demonstrates Lanier's gift for lyrical melody.

The second example of Lanier's vocal composition is *The Song of Love and Death* or *The Song of Elaine* (as it is entitled on the music manuscript), from "Lancelot and Elaine" in *Idylls of the King.*[17] This was one of Lanier's favorite poetic works, and he even quoted from it (among many other literary pieces) in *Tiger-Lilies.* Lanier had written to his brother from his barracks in 1862, asking for the verses: "I suppose you have Tennyson's Idylls of the King with you—If so, I wish you'd copy for me the little song which I have admired so much. . . . Copy [the verses] off and send them to me, as early as possible—I'm going to try and set them to music."[18] But the business of war intervened, and not until more than three years later could he announce to Clifford: "Have a new song out for soprano voice, Music by me, and words by Tennyson, the 'Sweet is true love, Tho' given in vain, in vain.' &c."[19] The song is a quaint example of inappropriate setting; the

---

[17]Original manuscript, Charles D. Lanier Papers, John Work Garrett Library.

[18]Lanier, "To Clifford A. Lanier," 18 January 1862, CE, 7:50-51.

[19]Lanier, "To Clifford A. Lanier," 30 September 1865, ibid., 200.

music itself is pretty, but does not quite fit the tone of the lyrics. The singer is comparing the sweetness of love to that of death; but though she "would follow love, if that could be," she is compelled "to follow death, who calls for me." "Let me die" are the concluding words. Yet the music is overly sweet, the melody almost sprightly; the chordal accompaniment on the piano is broken by light runs between lines which disturb whatever serious tone can be conveyed. Where the lyrics conclude with a resigned finality, Lanier's setting ends almost in triumph. From a purely musical stand-point, *The Song of Elaine* is pleasing in terms of its melodic flow, but with respect to treatment of lyrics, it is less than successful.

There are three other songs by Lanier that remain—all settings of Tennyson. Whereas there is the possibility that they may belong to the "four somewhat elaborate pieces of music" that Lanier sent from Prattville to a New Orleans publisher in 1868,[20] it is doubtful that these songs were written that early, for there is too much disparity between the immaturity of *Little Ella* and these more studied efforts. At least two of these were definitely written prior to September 1871, for Mary Day Lanier mentions them in a letter to her husband, who had just left for New York to consult a physician. "Last evening, at the piano," she wrote, "I came across thy song 'Love which hath us in the net,' and Miss Mary tried it. . . . She despaired of ever memorizing in so short a time, the 'Break, Break!' accompaniment, or would—I think—have liked that even better."[21] Lanier's third Tennyson song, *Flow Down, Cold Rivulet*, may have been written during the same period as the others, but this is uncertain.

These three songs reflect marked musical sophistication: Lanier's maturation is obvious. The least reliable indicator of Lanier's skills, however—but the most melodic of the songs—is *Love That Hath Us in the Net*. There is no manuscript available; the 1883 version is published and arranged by A. E. Blackmar, and there is no way of knowing exactly what changes, if any, he made (perhaps he added the guitar line to the vocal and piano lines). But the song is a piece of gentle lyricism, truly, as Blackmar inscribed on the sheet-music cover, "A Little Song Gem."

---

[20]Lanier, "To Robert S. Lanier," 7 April 1868, ibid., 381.

[21]Mary Day Lanier to Sidney Lanier, 20 September 1871, Charles D. Lanier Papers.

Break, Break, Break lives up to its title in its somewhat fragmented composition. Though only fifty-three measures in length, it contains four distinct sections (and three key changes) which connect, musically, in an abrupt and awkward manner. Its lack of smoothness seems to indicate a self-consciousness in Lanier's attempts to convey a different motif for each description within the lyrics. There are three elements in the narrative line: the description of the sea crashing against the shore, which contrasts with the innocent joy of the fisherman's children and the sailor, which in turn contrasts with the narrator's grief for a loved one now departed. The narrator is detached, observing both the carefree play of the young and the impersonal, relentless force of nature.

Lanier matched each vignette to a separate musical pattern in a way that is both admirable and inappropriate. Pounding chords on the piano open the song and continue as the singer enters; the steady, driving—almost sinister—chords reflect the force of the sea, creating a somber mood. When the children are depicted, their happiness is actually poignant, for the narrator perceives it through his own sorrow. But Lanier switches the musical mood completely, giving this section a lilting, flowing quality through the use of arpeggios on the piano. The transition to the next section is accomplished by a key change—slightly jarring to the ear—and a sudden switch from flowing figures to majestic chords. This is Lanier's weakest point in terms of the construction of the piece; the bridge passages sound artificial and disturb the continuity of the song. This third section, in which "the stately ships go on, / To their haven under the hill," is a modified march, indeed stately, with steady but clipped chords in the accompaniment. But the next lines, which are a direct contrast of mood— "But oh for the touch of a vanished hand, / And the sound of a voice that is still"—are given the same treatment. It cannot work. The piano then returns to the driving chords of the opening to introduce the conclusion of the song, which is in the home key; only this section is unified with regard to appropriate musical setting for the words. But the faults of *Break, Break, Break* are far fewer than those of *Little Ella* or *The Song of Elaine*. The faults of this later work are not the product of immaturity but of ambition—challenging a difficult text with inadequate musical skills.

Most satisfying of all is *Flow Down, Cold Rivulet*, in which the singer bids farewell to a stream, contrasting its permanence with his own transitory nature. Movement of water is suggested by an undulating figure in the bass line of the piano:

The repetition of this figure establishes an undercurrent of increasing motion that reaches a crest of pulsating sixteenth notes as the stream gains force:

Fitting the musical motion to the sense of the text is further enhanced in the second line of each verse by the use of chromatic lines, descending in the vocal part and ascending in the accompaniment. This figure appropriately depicts a wave in the first verse and quivering moonbeams in the second. Although the song is wistful and sad in tone, as a composition it is a happy example of Lanier at his best, fitting the correct type of music to the words, and creating, through the use of repeated motifs, a clear and unified whole.

Lanier's songs demonstrate a more than common talent; his melodies are intriguing, always moving in ways the ear does not expect, but always with a definite sensitivity to beauty. But these songs do not indicate musical genius, and it is very doubtful that a reputation could have been founded solely upon works like these. They are fascinating now because they are curiosities, in the same way that a rather ordinary eighteenth-century string quartet is fascinating when it is discovered that the composer is Benjamin Franklin.[22] Lanier's songs, too, might be considered mediocre by strict aesthetic standards, but a fair appraisal will find them charming, entertaining, and indicative of a substantial talent waiting to be developed.

The three compositions that won Lanier much praise during his lifetime, and upon which a good part of his contemporary reputation as a flutist was based, are *Black-birds* (or *Field-larks and Black-birds*), *Danse des Moucherons*, and *Wind-Song*. Each exemplifies Lanier's devotion to nature as a source of inspiration, perhaps in recollection of his childhood days when he wandered through the woods and along the banks of the Ocmulgee River in Macon, playing his one-keyed flute. Each of these pieces is programmatic in design, revealing Lanier's technical playing skills as well as his strengths and weaknesses as a composer.

Isabel Dobbin, who played in the Peabody orchestra with Lanier, writes that, during one of their concerts, Hamerik decided to have Lanier display his soloistic qualities and asked him to play *Black-birds*; this Lanier did, and with "wonderful trills and roulades and soulful melodies completely captivated" the audience.[23] The critic for the Baltimore *Gazette*, Innes Randolph, reported how Lanier "played without accompaniment his 'Blackbirds.' It is an imitative piece, suggesting strongly the song of the Blackbird, and showing a very fine technical mastery of the instrument. In one part, he carried a theme accompanied by the roll of deep arpeggios below that was very fine."[24] The extant fragmentary version of *Black-birds* consists mainly of delicate arpeggios.

Lanier's next attempt at programme music resulted in *Danse des Moucherons* (or Midge-dance), written in December 1873, just after he had

---

[22]Benjamin Franklin, *Quartet, three violins and viola and cello, F major*. Performed by members of the Royal Philharmonic, London (New York: Society for the Preservation of the American Musical Heritage, 1965). Franklin is generally believed to be the composer of this piece.

[23]Isabel L. Dobbin, "Lanier at the Peabody," *Peabody Bulletin* (April-May 1911): 4.

[24]Article of 8 December 1873, quoted in Richard Higgins, "Sidney Lanier, Musician" (dissertation, Peabody Conservatory of Music, 1969).

first settled himself in Baltimore. The manuscript is inscribed: "To Henry C. Wysham. Dec. 25, 1873." Lanier first mentioned the piece in a letter to his wife in February 1874: "I am copying off,—in order to try the publishers therewith—a *Danse des Moucherons* (Midge-dance) wh. I have written for flute and piano, and wh. I think enough of to let it go forward as Op. 1. Dost thou remember one morning last summer, Charley and I were walking in the upper part of the yard, before breakfast, and saw a swarm of gnats, of whose strange evolutions we did relate to thee a marvellous tale? I have put the grave oaks, the quiet shade, the sudden sunlight, the fantastic, contrariwise and ever-shifting midge-movements, the sweet hills afar off, and *thee* with thy earnest wide eyes,—all in the piece, and thus *I* like it: but I know not if others will, I have not played it for anybody."[25]

It is significant that Lanier considered this piece his "Opus 1"—consigning all earlier pieces, including his one published song, *Little Ella*, the works written in San Antonio, and even the recent *Black-birds*, to a period of preparation and, perhaps, artistic immaturity. This statement was Lanier's declaration that he realized he had reached an important point of demarcation in his life; he now recognized his previous musical compositions as exercises, student-pieces, juvenilia. With the beginning of his Baltimore period, he also began anew as a true artist and could now move into more complex and inventive musical forms.

Lanier may initially have been shy about his new work, but apparently thought enough of it to try, by September 1874, to have it published in New York. The following January he planned to arrange the "gnat-dance" as a symphony "for orchestra with flute *obligato*."[26] However, both of these projects came to nothing.

Danse des Moucherons is perhaps the most satisfying of Lanier's instrumental pieces. Unlike *Black-birds*, this work has an overall framework, a unity derived from the introduction and repetition of two distinct themes. It is also the piece about whose programmatic nature Lanier was most conscious. On a copy dedicated to Frederick H. Gottlieb by Lanier's family, these more complete notes by Lanier are inscribed:

---

[25]Lanier, "To Mary Day Lanier," 12 February 1874, CE, 9:31-32.

[26]Lanier, "To Mary Day Lanier," 3 January 1875, ibid., 135.

Early on a warm morning of last summer, Charley and I were walking in the dense shadow of some noble oaks, in Georgia, when suddenly the rising sun shot a ray thru the leaves, which illuminated the festivities of a swarm of midges.

The dance of these careless little creatures was at once perplexing, graceful & fascinating. Each midge seemed to have his own little space, within which he moved *ad libitum*: yet he always preserved such limits as would not interfere with the general outline of the wonderfully precise figures which the entire mass of midges were continually describing in endless variety,—playing much the same part that a man does in the great Plan of Life.

They advanced, retreated, swayed hither & thither, expanded into a large sphere, contracted into a small one, described figures of arches, columns, squares, & the like; and, sometimes,—as if by a signal communicated with the rapidity of lightning from the topmost to the lowest—they would all descend & disappear on the ground—like a beautifully played chromatic scale running down into silence.

This piece is a translation of the same.[27]

The music does fulfill the programme in many respects. The flute flight of the gnats, no matter how it moves *ad libitum*, is always grounded by chords on the piano. The flight always moves within a fixed area; its freedom of movement is checked before it moves out of its designated realm, and it returns to a lower, more conservative level. The sweeping travel of the gnats begins slowly:

The flute then breaks away from the piano for a cadenza-like passage, rejoining it for an allegretto in 3/8. Here the flight rises gradually in a series of figures in sixteenths:

---

[27]Manuscript copy, Charles D. Lanier Papers, John Work Garrett Library. The handwriting appears to be that of Mary Day Lanier. Gottlieb was a Baltimore businessman who replaced Wysham in the Peabody orchestra after the latter left for California in 1879.

but it never drifts too far from either the first tempo or the home key. A second, more deliberate motif is brought in (perhaps this is the "large sphere" described by the gnats now "contracted into a small one"):

After a series of descending sixteenths, the figures in theme B (allegretto) are repeated, followed by a return to the *meno mosso*. The flute has a cadenza of descending chromatics, though not quite "running down into silence," for the piano rejoins it for a lively ending. The piece as a whole is melodic, unified, and has definite direction. The flute part requires technical dexterity, but the piano accompaniment is just that—accompaniment. For the most part, the piano plays chords or parallels the flute; polyphonic writing seems to have been beyond Lanier's domain. His friend Ronald McDonald, who wrote for the *New York Times*, reported that this piece, "in its light and brilliant structure rivals the famed 'Queen Mab' scherzo of Berlioz,"[28] but a more objective critic can appreciate it as a simple, satisfying piece that successfully evokes the images projected in its programme.

Wind-Song represents a more ambitious endeavor; Gilbert Chase thought this 125-measure flute solo "is certainly worthy of being included in the permanent repertoire of American music for flute."[29] Lanier was probably in San Antonio when the idea of capturing the wind in music

---

[28]Quoted in CE, 7:xxi.

[29]Chase, *America's Music*, 344.

first occurred to him; a sheet of manuscript paper marked with "Dec. 27th 1872" and the name of that city contains seven fragmentary measures of a "Wind-song." This initial effort was probably revised and finished while Lanier was in Georgia during the summer of 1874. However, since the completed version does not resemble this fragment, it is more likely that Lanier simply rethought the idea of a wind-song and started fresh. It was finished in time for him to take it to New York in the fall of 1874, and on 29 October he played it for Leopold Damrosch, one of the country's most prominent musicians. Although he acknowledged that "it was done like an Artist" and he praised "the poetry of the piece,"[30] Damrosch evidently did not do anything tangible for Lanier as a result.

Nor does *Wind-Song* appear to have brought Lanier any fame as a composer. The piece, if its intent was to capture the ineffable sound of the wind, comes close to the mark, for there is no sense of anything solid or substantial in it. There is no single motif or melody, but one continuous line drifting from section to section. *Wind-Song* is a series of figures—mostly arpeggios and chromatic scales—rather than a series of themes. Apparently, Lanier's execution of the piece had a great deal to do with its success; consummate skill is certainly required to make *Wind-Song* the ethereal embodiment Lanier intended and not just a progression of exercises. Although this is not as memorable or "singable" as *Danse des Moucherons*, it does represent, as an exhibition piece, his breaking with simplicity and conventionality. This is Lanier's equivalent of a foray into the avant-garde.

His basic lack of preparedness, however, in the technical aspects of music—counterpoint, harmony, instrumentation, or orchestration—prohibited Lanier from working in more complex compositional forms. Notebooks kept by Lanier indicate that he was aware of such musical elements as diatonic scales and chordal progressions,[31] but he apparently did not have any advanced training in composition. Much has been made of Lanier's "symphonies" by critics. John Tasker Howard and George Kent Bellows in *A Short History of Music in America* and Gilbert Chase in *America's Music* mention Lanier's "three unfinished symphonies": *Symphony of the Plan-*

---

[30]Lanier, "To Mary Day Lanier," 29 October 1874, CE, 9:110.

[31]These notebooks are among the Charles D. Lanier Papers, John Work Garrett Library.

tation, *Choral Symphony*, and *Symphony of Life*.[32] This unfortunately raises the hopes of those American musicologists who wish to discover in Lanier a composer of unrecognized or unfulfilled genius. He was indeed unfulfilled, for as Chase points out, if Lanier had simply lived longer he might have learned enough to enable him to complete these works. But the extant musical fragments indicate only talent, not genius. There is a substantial distinction between "unfinished" symphonies and those hardly begun.

Only fragments of these "symphonies" exist in manuscript, the most extensive of which is *Symphony of Life*, and the evidence it presents borders on the pathetic. Lanier planned the usual four-movement structure, with each representing a phase of the life-cycle: "Childhood, Youth, Manhood, Death." He apparently prepared large sheets of manuscript paper, dutifully inscribing each movement title at the head of a page, and attempted to write. Unfortunately, he was unable to compose more than a few measures in each "movement," and these are scored for only one or two instruments. The fourth movement, for instance, consists of only four measures—for tympani.[33] Lanier simply did not possess compositional technique sufficient to write for an entire orchestra or even to sustain a musical idea for a prolonged piece.

Actually, he seems to have been concerned with these symphonies only towards the end of his life, perhaps because he was waiting to hear as much music as he could before attempting any very complex compositional work of his own. In a letter of 12 February 1881, Lanier mentions "things I am waiting to do, many of them half-done," including "my *Choral Symphony*, for chorus and Orchestra, being my Psalm of the West, with music . . . my Symphony *Life*, in four movements . . . my *Symphony of the Plantation*, being the old and new life of the negro in music . . . my *Symphony of the Woods*,—all these symphonies lying in chaos now about my memorandum-books."[34] His severely deteriorating health also had a great deal to do with his lack of attention to this composition work. But the major reason, the most obviously documented reason, was that he had turned to

---

[32]Howard and Bellows, *A Short History of Music*, 143; Chase, *America's Music*, 344.

[33]Original manuscript, Charles D. Lanier Papers, John Work Garrett Library.

[34]Lanier, "To Sarah J. Farley," 12 February 1881, CE, 10:289-90.

poetry as his primary creative objective. For in 1874, the same year he played his first season at the Peabody and composed his "Op. 1," Lanier also wrote his first poem that gained popular acclaim: *Corn*.

CHAPTER VI

1874:
Conflict and Triumph

IT WAS NOW 1874, and critics of Lanier agree with the poet himself that this year was the crucial turning point of his career. For the first time, he was earning a salary as a musician and was reasonably established within an artistic milieu. Such security allowed Lanier to direct his attention toward literature.

However, this luxury rekindled conflict within him. Having irrevocably resolved the inner turmoil to pursue the arts, he now had to decide which muse would dominate—that of music or that of poetry. Whereas he ultimately saw himself as writer and scholar, at this point—at the beginning of his Baltimore period—he was so enraptured by his good fortune that he had difficulty channeling his feverish energy in a single direction. This period of total immersion in the aesthetic life clarified his creative ideas and shaped the poetry upon which his modern reputation is primarily based. But Lanier's emotions were constantly warring with his intellect for control, and he always responded to music on an emotional level, even to the point of obsession. For him, music was not only an intellectual-artistic discipline; it was a controlling life force.

An additional element of stress was his lack of formal musical training. Lanier was not unaware of this handicap; after having played with the Peabody orchestra for just a few weeks, he called "this Orchestral business" a "tremendous trial of patience": "Having had no musical education whatever, knowing nothing save what I had 'picked up' in the most desultory way, unacquainted even with the meaning of a Conductor's motions,—and at the same time suddenly saddled with the duty of interpreting a responsible part in works which I had never even heard before, in company, too, with old musicians most of whom have been playing ever since they were children and doing nothing else,—all this nearly made my spirit give way many times."[1] But six days after this outburst, typical Lanierian optimistic fantasizing had once again gained control: "Now,—in thine ear," he wrote to his wife, "of all the ears in the world, be it whispered,— I could conduct a concert far, far better than this one. How well I now understand the foundation which music has, in the culture of the soul!"[2]

Between these extremes of self-criticism and self-exaltation, Lanier did develop professionally in positive ways; his excitement over what he thought he could accomplish should not be interpreted as braggadocio, but rather as symptomatic of the enthusiasm with which he embraced all things of beauty. At first Lanier may have doubted his musical talents, but they apparently improved steadily so that he not only kept pace with the rest of the orchestra, but excelled in his position. It would have been impossible for Lanier to have been allowed—by conductor, fellow musicians, press, or public—to continue if his playing were sloppy or his intonation poor. In fact, during one of Lanier's first concerts, his solo work in a section of Rossini's *William Tell* overture was acknowledged when "the audience broke into applause wh. was only stilled by the continuance of the overture: and the Conductor came down and said it was beautifully played."[3] This display of skill was also noted in the local papers.

During this early period in the orchestra, Lanier matured in outlook and technique: "How much I have learned in the last two months! I am not yet an artist, though on the flute. . . . I wd. not call myself a virtuoso within a year."[4] This was characteristic behavior: he wanted to do everything he had seen, to play everything he had heard, yet was constantly aware that he had to temper his enthusiasm with a scholar's patience.

---

[1]Sidney Lanier, "To Clifford A. Lanier," 4 January 1874, in *The Centennial Edition of the Works of Sidney Lanier*, ed. Charles R. Anderson et al., 10 vols. (Baltimore: Johns Hopkins Press, 1945) 9:8 (hereafter cited as CE).

[2]Lanier, "To Mary Day Lanier," 10 January 1874, ibid., 12.

[3]Lanier, "To Mary Day Lanier," 7 February 1874, ibid., 27.

[4]Ibid.

Sustained by the security and self-confidence gained in the orchestra, Lanier could now devote more effort to developing as a poet. His pre-1874 poems followed the song-concept, being balladic in form, repetitive, and simple in structure if not always in idea. But Lanier's development as a professional musician—his experience of hearing many instrumental voices simultaneously, intertwining melodic lines, his flute not a solo but one part of the entire ensemble, and the developed, rather than repeated, ideas of a symphony—enabled him to begin writing poems of increasing intellectual and textural complexity.

As an example, the first two stanzas of an 1863 poem, *Resurrection*, can be compared with the beginning of the 1874 *Corn*. *Resurrection* consists of seven stanzas of iambic pentameter lines with an ABAB rhyme scheme, one of the most common poetic forms. Its beat is insistent but monotonous (only one line is not end-stopped); there is little contrast in word-sounds or duration:

> *Sometimes, in morning sunlights by the river,*
> *Where in the early fall long grasses wave,*
> *Light winds from over the moorland sink and shiver*
> *And sigh as if just blown across a grave.*
>
> *And then I pause and listen to this sighing,*
> *And look with strange eyes on the well-known stream,*
> *And hear wild birth-cries uttered by the dying,*
> *And know men waking who appear to dream.* [5]

Corn is far more arresting, with its varying line lengths, onomatopoeic effects, and judiciously used repetitions. There is still a strong beat, but there is also enough variation within the lines to prevent monotony. Although iambic pentameter is also the dominant metrical form, it never becomes intrusive, for there are run-on lines, shorter dactylic lines, and contrasting sounds within and between lines to generate a sense of motion. Whereas *Resurrection* speaks primarily to the mind, *Corn* also effectively addresses the senses:

---

[5]CE, 1:16.

> To-day the woods are trembling through and through
> With shimmering forms, that flash before my view,
> Then melt in green as dawn-stars melt in blue.
>> The leaves that wave against my cheek caress
>> Like women's hands; the embracing boughs express
>> A subtlety of mighty tenderness;
> The copse-depths into little noises start,
> That sound anon like beating of a heart,
> Anon like talk 'twixt lips not far apart.
>> The beech trees balm, as a dreamer hums a song;
>> Through that vague wafture, expirations strong
>> Throb from young hickories breathing deep and long
> With stress and urgence bold of prisoned spring
> And ecstasy of burgeoning. [6]

Corn was written during the summer of 1874, a period of rest and domestic serenity for Lanier. After the Peabody concert season had ended in
early April, he went on a short concert tour with several other Baltimore
musicians to West Virginia and Ohio, and was home in Georgia by May.
This was his first reunion with his family since the beginning of his Baltimore adventure.[7] He was also appearing for the first time in his native
city as a respected professional musician. At the end of May, Lanier joined
the Macon Harmonic Society in a performance during which, as the Macon *Telegraph* reported, he "held his audience in rapt attention, and a per-
sistent encore was the only means of relieving everybody."[8] He played with
them again a month later, contributing *Black-birds* to the program.

Lanier spent most of the summer with his family visiting friends in
Sunnyside, a small village between Macon and Atlanta. Here he could
rest, surrounded by his wife and sons, friends, and the Georgia countryside. Music was not forgotten, though. Lanier played the flute for hours

---

[6]Ibid., 34, ll. 1-14.

[7]Although Lanier was now being paid to play the flute, he was not paid much;
and the financial exigencies of living in Baltimore made it impossible for him to
uproot Mary and the boys and bring them north. Although this situation, which
lasted three years, was personally less than satisfying to the Laniers, the extensive, detailed, and loving correspondence that resulted is a valuable record of Lanier's experiences, which scholars would not have otherwise.

[8]Quoted in Aubrey Harrison Starke, *Sidney Lanier: A Biographical and Critical
Study* (reprint, New York: Russell and Russell, 1964) 181.

and "at all times of the day and night—walking up and down the roadway that ran beside the railroad track, oblivious of everything, even of the . . . boys who made flutes from swamp reeds and followed him, charmed children fascinated by the piper."[9]

Now that he was again within the physical reach of family, Lanier was expected to return to the law firm; however, his walks and meditations gave him time to think. Perhaps he was recalling the ethereal strains he had heard the previous winter in Baltimore—the melodies of Berlioz and Gade—such sounds he had never heard prior to playing at the Peabody. He could have been remembering the triumphs he had had as "flauto primo."

Music was once more victorious, as revealed in letters written shortly after his arrival home. On 26 May, Lanier wrote that "I took my old place in the law firm immediately on arrival [and] the terribly warm weather has completely wilted me, already: and it is now definitely and irrevocably decided that I am to quit the law."[10] After relating a brief outline of his Baltimore career to his friend, poet Paul Hamilton Hayne, he declared: " 'Tis quite settled that I cannot practice law: either writing or speaking appears to produce small haemorrages which completely sap my strength: and I am going in a few weeks to New York,—without knowing what on earth I am to do there—armed only with a Silver Boehm flute, and some dozen of steel pens."[11]

He spoke in stronger terms to his brother. He had returned to Macon "with the idea that my health was sufficiently restored to permit my resumption of my old place in the firm. . . . A few days of law-work and of this dreadful climate have demonstrated the absolute impossibility of my being a lawyer."[12] But was the "dreadful climate" and "poisonous atmosphere" debilitating only to Lanier's physical health?[13] Probably not. La-

---

[9]Ibid., 182.

[10]Lanier, "To Virginia Hankins," 26 May 1874, CE, 9:58.

[11]23 May 1874, ibid., 56-57.

[12]Lanier, "To Clifford A. Lanier," 28 May 1874, ibid., 59.

[13]This is in contrast to local claims that Macon's atmosphere was "invigorating and peculiarly adapted to consumptives and those otherwise afflicted by the vigorous colds of Northern climates." John C. Butler, *Historical Record of Macon and Central Georgia* (Macon: J. W. Burke, 1879) 289.

nier had had his taste of the big city, had lived with musicians, and had found a challenge. Macon—especially when seen from behind his law desk—had nothing to offer a man of his talent and temperament. Certainly the sultry climate could do nothing to benefit his health, but the vehemence with which he lashed out at the restrictions which Macon life would place upon him suggests that one motivation of his visit home was to prove that he could survive only in the art-life of a cosmopolitan environment.

At last Lanier had firmly decided upon the course of his life; whatever doubts he may have had were resolved by the Baltimore experience. "I've shed all the tears about it that I'm going to," he wrote, "and am now vigorously engaged in pumping myself full of music and poetry, with which I propose to water the dry world. I suppose it may now be finally said, that God had cut me off inexorably from any other life than this."[14] He told Clifford he would stay in Georgia for the summer, working on his long poem The Jacquerie (about a fourteenth-century peasant rebellion in France) and "a lot of music wh. I have nearly ready for the press,"[15] and then go to New York to find musical employment. By the time Lanier was ready to return to New York, he had, in addition to his flute and pens, the manuscript of Corn, and a revised version of Wind-Song. Both of these works would secure some success for Lanier, but it would be quite some time before he would receive anything resembling widespread popular recognition.

Lanier returned to New York and quickly resumed his former life of musical comradeship. The genuine joy in his letters reveals that the most important life to him was the artistic one. As soon as he was surrounded by music, listening to Thomas's orchestra, drinking beer with European musicians, and meeting his friends for informal recitals, his vitality was renewed. This enthusiasm was also reflected in a series of plans and projects, none of which, however, were to materialize, making this period seem, in retrospect, futile.

---

[14]Lanier, "To Clifford A. Lanier," 28 May 1874, CE, 9:59.

[15]Ibid., 60. After Little Ella was published in 1868, Lanier did not see any more of his music in print.

Letters written from New York through mid-November outline many ideas flowing through Lanier's mind. He had conceived of a new type of flute, one which "will go down to G below the Staff, and wh. will entirely remedy the imperfections which now exist in that part of the flute that extendeth below D." He dreamed of "an Orchestra in which shall be as many first flutes as first violins and as many second flutes as second violins. . . . I say this not out of my foolish advocacy of the flute . . . I speak in advocacy of pure music."[16]

While seeking publishers for his music and for *Corn*, he hoped to obtain a position translating a book on music by Rousseau; he also applied to several Southern newspapers, asking if they wished a correspondent in New York. None did. He planned "Soft-Tone concerts" in which he would present "Beethoven's great Octett for Oboes, Clarionets, & Flutes, some quartets & trios for flutes, solos on Bass-flute & Concert-flute."[17] Lanier apparently sketched some music for these concerts, but they were never held.

To his father, Lanier had to sound very grand. "I have a fair prospect of becoming musical and dramatic critic for a large Baltimore paper," he wrote. He also told his father how popular *Corn* was, and how it and his music would surely sell. His musical compositions, he added, were "so original, that I have, as all original writers must, to 'make my public': and this I am rapidly doing, by various influences which I have brought to bear, but which it would take me too long to detail."[18] The details were lacking because there probably were none; this is a letter from a man trying to justify himself to his father. Its tone is typical of Lanier's attitude: he was slow to accept defeat and just as eager to snatch at every wisp of possible success.

What a hopeful and yet pathetic time those months in New York must have been. In October, *Corn* was rejected by the *Atlantic Monthly*, whose editor, William Dean Howells, found Lanier's "worst danger is a vein of mysticism running through all he writes."[19] This blow was so defeating that

---

[16]Lanier, "To Mary Day Lanier," 3 September 1874, CE, 9:76.

[17]Lanier, "To Mary Day Lanier," 12 September 1874, ibid., 82-83.

[18]Lanier, "To Robert S. Lanier," 24 September 1874, ibid., 90.

[19]William Dean Howells to M. M. Hurd, 3 October 1874, ibid., 96.

Lanier never even mentioned it to his wife, with whom he shared all his thoughts, plans, and experiences; he later wrote about it to others. But to Mary and Clifford, Lanier wrote only of great things—that New York musicians continued to be impressed with his compositions. He continued to work on his new flute (until funds ran out); he intended to write a flute method-book to surpass the existing one; and he hoped to obtain a contract to translate *Das Rheingold*.

At the same time that Lanier was making these grandiose plans, he was also beginning to realize the futility of his quest in New York. In that city, particularly, he noted that "one must have the crust broken for him by some of the *Ins*, or he will remain forever *out*, if he were Beethoven and Wagner in one."[20] Although he had "several plans . . . in process of negotiation," he now saw that musical employment there was far from being a possibility: "I do not now think at all of getting into any Orchestra here: for the good reason that there is really no Orchestra to get into. Thomas' is the only one . . . and he had imported a flutist from Russia to fill his only vacancy, some three months before I came here."[21]

Lanier's jubilation at his first real opportunity—or appearance of opportunity—is therefore understandable. He was to play before maestro Leopold Damrosch, Thomas's great rival in New York. Like Thomas, Damrosch was a native of Germany and had been personally friends with Liszt, Wagner, and von Bülow.[22] In New York, he conducted the choral Männergesangverein Arion, beginning in 1871, and introduced the new German music to his audiences. In 1873 he organized the Oratorio Society of New York. He did this on the advice of the internationally acclaimed Russian pianist and composer, Anton Rubinstein, who was then touring America. Rubinstein recommended that conducting a major choral group was the only way Damrosch could hope to match Thomas, who already monopolized the orchestral market. The Oratorio Society flourished, as did the rivalry between the two conductors, and in 1878 Damrosch finally founded his own orchestra, which later joined the small

---

[20]Lanier, "To Clifford A. Lanier," 24 September 1874, ibid., 100.

[21]Lanier, "To Mary Day Lanier," 21 October 1874, ibid., 104.

[22]David Ewen, *Music Comes to America* (New York: Thomas Y. Crowell, 1942) 41.

Philharmonic orchestra to become the institution it is today.[23] As a supporter of the new music, Damrosch presented the American premieres of Berlioz's *Damnation of Faust*, Act III of *Siegfried* and Act I of *Die Walküre* by Wagner, and Brahms's *Symphony #1*.[24]

Damrosch was also Thomas's temperamental opposite. Thomas had a "sound practical sense . . . never lived long in a world of dreams," and was "matter of fact, rarely given to excessive enthusiasm, always calculating and controlled." Damrosch was warm, social, and idealistic: "He permitted his imagination free rein. By nature a romanticist, his head was often in the clouds. He could dream bold dreams, unhampered by sound practical considerations."[25] This description could easily fit Lanier, and perhaps the two men recognized in each other, if only briefly, a kindred spirit.

At a private recital in Brooklyn in September 1874, Lanier had impressed a Mr. Cortada, pianist "of the Oratorio Society of New York and of the Handel and Haydn Society of Brooklyn. . . . He declareth that I can do great things with a little study: and volunteereth to introduce me to Dr. Dammrosch [sic] (under whom he saith I must study)."[26] The week before, Lanier had written that John Cornell, organist of St. Paul's in New York, "is to take me to see Dr. Dammrosch, who appears to be the coming man at present."[27] Lanier apparently wanted to assure himself that he would, somehow, be granted this interview, having had so many possibilities constantly elude him. Lanier must have seen Damrosch conduct before their meeting, for on 25 September he wrote: "I am going to move heaven and earth for ways and means to take lessons from Dr. Dammrosch. . . . He is a beautiful violinist, and is considered at the head of fine music in New York. A slender blue-eyed man, with a broad forehead, is he: and a man of culture withal."[28]

---

[23]John Tasker Howard and George Kent Bellows, *A Short History of Music in America* (New York: Thomas Y. Crowell, 1957) 144-45.

[24]Ewen, *Music Comes to America*, 43. Brahms himself had wished Thomas to conduct his new symphony, but one of Damrosch's students managed to obtain a score, thereby robbing Thomas of a triumph.

[25]Ibid., 42.

[26]Lanier, "To Mary Day Lanier," 13 September 1874, CE, 9:82.

[27]Lanier, "To Mary Day Lanier," 8 September 1874, ibid., 78 n.88.

[28]Lanier, "To Mary Day Lanier," 25 September 1874, ibid., 91.

The long-anticipated meeting finally took place a month later, though whether through the offices of Cortada or Cornell is unclear. What matters is that Lanier at last had a chance to demonstrate two talents—playing and composing—before one of the country's great musical authorities. On 29 October, Lanier could proudly proclaim: "Today I played for the great Dr. Dammrosch:—and won him. I sang the Wind-Song to him. When I finished he came and shook my hand, and said it was done like an Artist: that it was wonderful, in view of my education: and that he was greatly astonished and pleased with the poetry of the piece and the enthusiasm of its rendering. He then closed the door to his next pupil, and kept him waiting in the front parlor a half hour, while giving me a long talk. . . . He is the only poet among the craft here: and is a thoroughly cultivated man, in all particulars. He offered to do all he could, in my behalf."[29] But all that Damrosch did was to have given Lanier these kind words (and a person of less dogged optimism might have even perceived discouragement in Damrosch's careful praise), although Lanier desperately needed some kindness.

But Asger Hamerik could do more. He still offered Lanier an actual job, which promised not only aid in "the dreadful struggle for bread,"[30] but also, as Lanier now knew, the opportunity for popular recognition. He returned to Georgia at the end of November, with the security of the Peabody position awaiting him once more. Receiving notice that *Scribner's* had accepted one of his sonnets and that *Lippincott's* would print *Corn*, it finally looked as though Lanier could realize his "daily-growing dream of authorship in music and poetry."[31]

Before returning to Baltimore, Lanier arranged a "Flute-fund concert" for the benefit of his stymied project on the improved flute. The concert was held in Macon's Harmonic Hall on 23 December 1874, with the assistance of several local musicians. Lanier and A. Huber played *Sounds from Home* for flute and zither. Three Macon ladies—Cora Hunter, Jessie Hardeman, and Carrie Boifeuiellet—performed songs, with Lanier providing a flute obligato for each. The program also included a piano duo,

[29]Lanier, "To Mary Day Lanier," 29 October 1874, ibid., 110.

[30]Lanier, "To Logan E. Bleckley," 15 November 1874, ibid., 121.

[31]Lanier, "To Clifford A. Lanier," 1 December 1874, ibid., 124.

Los Ojos Creoles, by Louis Moreau Gottschalk, and a solo delivered by Lanier, *Fantasie on Airs from Faust* by Garibaldi.[32] This was conventional concert fare, "chosen obviously with the Macon audience in mind."[33] But neither this strategy, nor some helpful publicity from the Macon *Telegraph and Messenger* helped make the concert a success. After the expenses had been covered, Lanier found he had come away with a profit of $1.20.

But this disappointment was eased shortly. Lanier left for Baltimore on Christmas morning, resumed his old seat in the Peabody orchestra, rented a piano so that he could compose more easily, and, on 17 January 1875, received definite word that *Corn* would soon be printed in *Lippincott's*. Not only did this carry with it a much-needed check for $50—it was the start of Lanier's national reputation as a poet.

---

[32]Original program, Charles D. Lanier Papers, John Work Garrett Library, the Johns Hopkins University, Baltimore, Maryland.

[33]Starke, *Sidney Lanier*, 197.

CHAPTER VII

1875:
Projects and Promise

IT APPEARED THAT LANIER had finally established his foothold in the artistic world. At the beginning of 1875, everything was right in his world, and he was surrounded by symbols of his success.

The Peabody orchestra, now a sizable ensemble of forty-four pieces, was giving glorious concerts under Asger Hamerik. He and Lanier had developed a special communication, being of like temperament, and they enjoyed long evenings of discussion and music-making. Society, in the form of musicians, the Danish consul, and the famous Baltimore piano manufacturer Knabe, was also taking an interest in Lanier, inviting him to soirees and champagne suppers.[1]

The triumphant publication of Corn brought fame and attention that would have lasting results. Lippincott's was a Philadelphia journal, and Corn was taken up by the literary people of that city, most notably by Gibson Peacock, editor of the Philadelphia Bulletin. He in turn sparked the interest of Charlotte Cushman, the venerable Shakespearean actress. She went to Baltimore at the end of January, summoned Lanier, and, after praising him, asked him to write a poem that she might read to her audiences.[2] She had thrilled the American and English stages in the 1840s and 1850s; now she

---

[1]Sidney Lanier, "To Mary Day Lanier," 24 January 1875, in The Centennial Edition of the Works of Sidney Lanier, ed. Charles R. Anderson et al., 10 vols. (Baltimore: Johns Hopkins Press, 1945) 9:146-47 (hereafter cited as CE).

[2]Aubrey Harrison Starke, Sidney Lanier: A Biographical and Critical Study (reprint, New York: Russell and Russell, 1945) 199.

was very ill, but, unwilling to give up her work entirely, she continued to greet her devoted followers as a platform reader. When she met Lanier, she found a kindred spirit in whom she saw many of her own ideals mirrored. When Lanier related his theory of poetry as sound, she remembered "an idea she had in 1840 about an article showing how a union of words and music might indicate the sighing of wind through the trees."[3] She also saw in Lanier a valiant fighter, a comrade, against disease; she had been suffering for years with cancer and could understand his drive to fulfill himself in art. In her sympathy with her friend's struggles, she forgot her own pain and became a champion of his work.[4]

Favorable reviews of *Corn* began to appear, but what especially pleased Lanier about its success was that it was "so cordially taken by the hand among the Northern people, in spite of its being so distinctly Georgian."[5] Although *Corn* was a "Southern" poem, it was not perceived as a regional work, and Lanier was, as he wished, regarded not as a Georgian poet but as an American poet. Perhaps the notice that gave him the most pleasure was Peacock's in the *Bulletin*, for in some measure it compensated for the hurt inflicted by William Dean Howells's rejection. Peacock called *Corn* the "most poetic of American poems," and "far superior to those three of Mr. Emerson's chosen Parnassians in the February *Atlantic*."[6] But Peacock was genuinely objective in praising its poetics, for he originally thought "Sidney Lanier" a pen-name and had no knowledge of Lanier at all. Peacock saw only that the author of *Corn* was a true poet.

With such laudation, Lanier began to conceive of himself as primarily a poet. He still occupied his first chair in the Peabody orchestra, often exhausted himself by dashing around Baltimore to play with a wind quintet or assist a string quintet, and occasionally sat at his piano, score-paper in hand, in a "fury of Creation."[7] But he would not actually complete any

---

[3]Joseph Leach, *Bright Particular Star: The Life and Times of Charlotte Cushman* (New Haven: Yale University Press, 1970) 382.

[4]Ibid., 383.

[5]Lanier, "To Logan E. Bleckley," 23 January 1875, CE, 9:145.

[6]Quoted in ibid., 147 n.25.

[7]Lanier, "To Mary Day Lanier," 12 January 1875, ibid., 139.

more musical compositions, for his attentions increasingly turned to poetic and academic interests.

Lanier's mania for "projects" took hold of him once more. In January, he had learned from the Peabody's librarian that the school had "a full set of apparatus for the physics of music lectures now at the Institute."[8] This sparked his hope of establishing—for himself—a professorship of the physics of music at the conservatory. If only he could persuade the trustees to allow him the use of this equipment for his experiments! At the end of the month, Professor Alfred F. Mayer of the Stevens Institute of Technology in New Jersey lectured on sound at the Peabody. Although Lanier recognized Mayer's scientific expertise—Lanier's review of the lecture series appeared in the Baltimore Gazette 5 February 1875—he found him "greatly hampered by the disadvantage of knowing nothing about music."[9] Lanier felt that he could give similar lectures, supplemented by his knowledge of music. He planned to accept Mayer's invitation to study at Stevens. "One month of daily service in his well-appointed laboratory would suffice to give me the manual dexterity in experimenting which I lack."[10] But he never did go.

He also hoped to go to Boston to study methods of teaching music and sight-reading ("wh. I design to suggest as part of the duties of my Chair"[11]) and then take the Peabody sound apparatus on a lecture tour of Georgia and Alabama. Finally, at the beginning of March, he obtained permission from the Peabody's Board of Trustees to use the equipment. On 14 March, he wrote excitedly to Clifford about his proposed series of forty lectures plus instruction in sight-reading and sight-singing, and asked him to arrange for a hall in Macon. He even mentioned what he wanted as a lecture fee. But two days later, he wrote to Mary that the whole project would have to be abandoned. One of the trustees, whom Lanier regarded as belonging to the "Opposition," informed him that they had "just torn down

---

[8]Lanier, "To Mary Day Lanier," 6 January 1875, ibid., 137.

[9]Lanier, "To Mary Day Lanier," 31 January 1875, ibid., 155.

[10]Ibid., 156.

[11]Ibid.

the building in which the musical department of the Institute had been carrying on its operations."[12]

However, something concrete was offered Lanier, which he accepted, but at the cost of pride and a great deal of physical pain. His new reputation as a writer inspired the Atlantic Coast Line Railroad, whose offices were in Baltimore, to commission him to write a guidebook for railroad travelers to Florida. The railroad offered to pay expenses and $125 a month—a contrast to the monthly $60 he made as a principal player in the Peabody orchestra. But the offer was, from an aesthetic standpoint, distasteful. "Well," Lanier wrote to his wife, "Apollo was a swineherd. . . . Shall I twist my nose at bread and meat?"[13] At this point, he needed income more immediately than reputation.

The travels for the volume were supposed to have occupied three months but took twice that time. At the end of the spring concert season Lanier made a short visit home, and then traveled to Jacksonville, St. Augustine, the Gulf Coast, the Everglades, and Key West. The guidebook was published by the firm of J. B. Lippincott in November 1875 and was a financial success. But to Lanier it had been "like a wound . . . ever since I was engaged to write it . . . I did not wish ever to appear before the public again save in the poetic character."[14] He tried to spare himself from the total prostitution of writing a potboiler (and he would have to write several others in order to make a living) by injecting as much of himself as he could into the prose. Therefore his descriptive passages are often very poetic: "surely no one with an eye either for agricultural advantages or for the more spiritual beauties of hill-curves and tree-arabesques can do other than praise the happiness of their choice";[15] "the hill-pines . . . stand upon the corrugations of the earth's brow. They represent pain, spasms, paroxysms, desperations. . . . they stand, distinct units, ranged in circles, in squares, and rhomboid figures, in endless aisles, in myriad-fold ranks, almost making a continuity by mere multitude."[16] This pleased many read-

---

[12]Lanier, "To Mary Day Lanier," 16 March 1875, ibid., 178-79.

[13]24 March 1875, ibid., 183.

[14]Lanier, "To Laura N. Boykin," 12 February 1876, ibid., 317.

[15]Lanier, *Florida*, CE, 6:70.

[16]Ibid., 48-49.

ers, but displeased others, including the reviewer for the Chicago *Tribune*, who found *Florida* a "serviceable guide-book" despite Lanier's "frequent fits of frenzied raving."[17]

The most poignant aspect of *Florida*, aside from the precious time and strength it stole from Lanier, is chapter 14: "For Consumptives." Describing himself as conducting "a desperate but to all appearances successful struggle with a case of consumption," he enumerated the many treatments for this "unknown blood-poison," including the "milk cure, the beef-blood cure, the grape cure, the raw-beef cure, the whisky cure, the health-lift cure,"[18] and, pertinent to the book, travel to a favorable climate such as that of Florida. He also mentioned his own favored treatment, "though there may be physicians who would oppose it": flute playing. The chapter is pathetic not only for its pitiful nineteenth-century ignorance of tuberculosis but because it is a record of the uselessness of Lanier's struggles.

But the spring of 1875 had not been totally sacrificed for *Florida*. Lanier had also written, rather quickly, a poem twice as long as *Corn* and containing many things which he had "very long wanted to say."[19] This work was *The Symphony*, which "took hold of me like a real James River Ague: and I have been in a mortal shake with the same, day and night, ever since. . . . It verily racks all the bones of my spirit." He explained briefly that in *The Symphony* each personified orchestral instrument would discuss "various deep social questions of the times, in the progress of the music."[20] *Lippincott's* magazine took the poem immediately, and it appeared in the June issue.

The Symphony was Sidney Lanier's protest of the industrial age undermining all that was beautiful in life. Like John Ruskin, he aligned social reform and artistic activities.[21] The problem of dealing with the negative aspects of civilization—unfair trade, exploitation, poverty—had long disturbed Lanier. As a student he had asked himself, "What is the province

[17]Quoted in CE, 6:xvii.

[18]*Florida*, ibid., 141-42.

[19]Lanier, "To Mary Day Lanier," 28 March 1875, CE, 9:184.

[20]Lanier, "To Gibson Peacock," 24 March 1875, ibid., 187.

[21]Starke, *Sidney Lanier*, 205.

of music in the economy of the world?" In his maturity, he saw music and the economy of the world working, in human terms, at cross purposes. Trade, with its inherent evils, would destroy civilization—unless the spiritual powers of Art could overcome it and thereby save mankind.

A letter Lanier wrote to his wife a year earlier revealed the anger he felt at the iniquity of trade. In April 1874, Lanier and several other Baltimore musicians visited Wheeling, West Virginia, on a short concert tour. He found this city to be a representation of Mammon, where "an eternal shower of soot drizzles downward in dismal disgust (wh. alliteration wellnigh tempteth the writer thereof to supplement the same with two more d's connected by a dash)." Wheeling represented the industrial world in microcosm, a frightening prospect to someone like Lanier, who believed that "it cannot be well, that a hundred men should die in soul and body, in order that one man should live merely in body."[22] Since living in the North, Lanier had enjoyed its cultural life, but had also witnessed the results of its mills and factories. Even his own chosen path indicated the injustice of the economic system; why should the life of art and scholarship be poor, while that of trade be luxuriant?

The Symphony is not a bitter diatribe, for though it cries angrily against the ways that trade has perverted mankind, it concludes in a spirit of hope and reconciliation. It is true to Lanier's own description—a poem in which various instruments discuss social questions—but it is not a poem in symphonic form. Much has been made of this, and attempts to analyze The Symphony in terms of musical composition have proved fruitless. But it is definitely a musician's poem. Only an experienced musician could be sensitive to the "commingling tunes"[23] of an orchestral piece and understand the contribution of each instrumental voice. And only a musician would assign such cosmic significance to the role of music.

In a series of solos, several instruments express their hatred of the exploiter Trade, which is "only war grown miserly" (l. 60). The sections have little to do with the sounds of the instruments, but Lanier does make an effort to embody the nature of the instrument in each part. The most spiritual solo, which sings of the union of nature and love as the hope of humankind, is therefore given to the flute. The "bold straightforward horn"

---

[22]Lanier, "To Mary Day Lanier," 16 April 1874, CE, 9:50.

[23]The Symphony, CE, 1:46-56. This reference is from line 335.

(l. 253) takes up the battle against Trade in chivalric terms; this section is ballad-like in construction. But the poem as an entirety is not symphonic in structure, although it does have a major unifying theme. Rather than consisting of movements, each following a pattern as dictated by the composition of a traditional symphony, Lanier's work consists of variations on a theme.

Its construction is similar to Lanier's flute piece *Wind-Song*, in which a series of musical figures—united but not internally developed—suggest the movement of the wind. Both *Wind-Song* and *The Symphony* indicate that at this point in his work Lanier was still operating within an experimental stage; he was using music to suggest intangible movement and poetry to suggest music, but had not yet developed one satisfactory mode in which he could comfortably express his ideal of the union of the arts.

There are evidences in *The Symphony* of Lanier's attempts to go beyond poetry to the evocation of the senses in synaesthetic effect. The section on the plight of the poor "that stand by the inward-opening door" is repeated (ll. 23, 192), with the variation, which provides the effect of a choral refrain. The instrumental sounds are depicted in terms of sensation. The flute sound is "velvet" and "half song, half odor" (l. 96); the clarinet tone is "melting" (l. 216); and the oboe plays and smiles (l. 326).

The concluding section, sung by the bassoons over the "commingling tunes" of the other instruments, describes life itself as a musical metaphor; life is a "sea-fugue, writ from east to west" (l. 347), and only love can make sense of the blotted and erased notes of the score. The discords produced by Trade, poverty, and callousness can be resolved only by Love. Love is the ascendant power, and *The Symphony* concludes in a tone of affirmation—though Lanier might have created something more appropriately triumphant than the chanting of bassoons, perhaps giving this section to the brass. But Love will finally be heard throughout the world, for over "the modern waste a dove hath whirred: Music is Love in search of a word." These famous concluding lines embody Lanier's three major concerns: music, united with love, is a force greater than the mere word.

The Symphony was even more successful than *Corn*, and with it Lanier's literary reputation was secure. It was published in the June 1875 issue of *Lippincott's* and reprinted in *Dwight's Journal of Music*. Enthusiastic reviews appeared in several newspapers, both in the North and South. Gibson Peacock excitedly contacted Bayard Taylor, a critic, poet, and one of the most eminent figures in New York literary society. In response,

Taylor wrote a warm letter to Lanier, inviting him to the New York celebration of Goethe's 126th birthday. He wrote: "I am heartily glad to welcome you to the fellowship of authors, so far as I may dare to represent it;
but, knowing the others, I venture to speak in their names also."[24] This
was the beginning of a very friendly correspondence, through which Taylor served Lanier by offering poetic criticism. Taylor was the most eminent literary man who was to assist Lanier; a year later, he would be
instrumental in securing for Lanier the commission to write the cantata
for the American centennial exercises.

When *The Symphony* appeared, Lanier was in the South working on
Florida. At the end of July, he went to New York for a month in order to
complete and revise the work. This time, he had solid ammunition with
which to assault the barricades of the city. He had the backing of Taylor,
and a letter of introduction to the chairman of the board of trustees of the
New York College of Music from the man's sister, sculptor Emma Stebbins, a close friend of Charlotte Cushman. "I am going to see if they will
found a chair of the Physics of Music," Lanier wrote to Peacock, "and give
it to me."[25]

A month later he was still planning to win the position. "I have some
valuable introductions to start on" at the College of Music, he wrote to
Clifford, "and the thing may succeed. If it does,—life will have perma-
nently arranged itself for me: and I won't have anything to do for the bal-
ance of it save to talk of music and write poetry."[26] But life would not oblige
Lanier with such a neat arrangement; in October, Colonel Stebbins informed him that the question of his position had to be postponed due to
"legal complications which have intervened."[27]

On 28 August, Lanier attended the Goethe commemoration at Gil-
more's Garden in Manhattan, and here, for the first time, he joined the
company of literary leaders. He sat in Bayard Taylor's box, where the two
were joined by William Cullen Bryant, who had come to deliver an ora-
tion. In October, Taylor took Lanier to the Century Association, a de-

---

[24]Letter of 17 August 1875, CE, 9:234 n.132.

[25]Lanier, "To Gibson Peacock," 31 July 1875, ibid., 226.

[26]Lanier, "To Clifford A. Lanier," 26 September 1875, ibid., 249.

[27]Lanier, "To Mary Day Lanier," 12 October 1875, ibid., 257.

scendant of the Bread-and-Cheese and Sketch Clubs of the Knickerbockers. To Lanier, the monthly meeting of the club, attended by the New York "illuminati," was "an Arabian Night," an initiation to "the delight of meeting and of conversing with thoughtful men and artists of many sorts."[28] Here he met Governor Samuel J. Tilden, editor Whitelaw Reid of the *New York Times*, sculptor John Quincy Adams Ward, painter Daniel Huntington, and poets Richard Henry Stoddard and Edmund C. Stedman. The excitement generated in Lanier by the meeting is reflected in a long exuberant letter to his wife. Here was the society he craved and in which he was even being made welcome. His spirits had not been so elevated in a long while; with Edmund Stedman's promised help to secure some book-reviewing work for *Scribner's* magazine, *Lippincott's* commission of a series of sketches of India, and the constant ministrations of the "good Caliph" Bayard Taylor, it seemed that permanent success for Lanier was near. "It really begins to look, now," he wrote, "as if there were some sign of steady and profitable employment for me in the work that I love."[29] This work was no longer music, but writing; the success of *Corn* and *The Symphony* had changed his orientation. As a musician, Lanier had never had much more than a local reputation, but as a poet he was now known to the entire nation. This recognition swayed his allegiance to writing, and he came to regard playing in the Peabody Orchestra as a "last resort."[30]

The efforts of the Florida travels had severely strained Lanier's health. He began to suffer more hemorrhages and moved from Brooklyn to the Westminster Hotel in Manhattan in order to spare himself the tiring ferry trip across the East River. By late fall, his health having improved, Lanier was able to go to Boston and visit Charlotte Cushman, who was nearing the end of her strength. Lanier had been corresponding with her, but it was through Gibson Peacock that she was informed of Lanier's health, about which she was continually concerned.

Lanier arrived in the snowy city on 2 November and went to the Parker House hotel, where Miss Cushman was a resident, to find that she had

---

[28]Lanier, "To Mary Day Lanier," 4 October 1875, ibid., 253.

[29]Ibid., 255.

[30]Lanier, "To Mary Day Lanier," 12 October 1875, ibid., 258.

had his room prepared and warmed with a coal-fire. In the middle of wash-
ing, Lanier heard "a merry tap at my door—and on opening the same, the
face of my veritable Charlotte—whom I had expected to find all propped
up in pillows—glowing."[31] He joined Miss Cushman in her parlor for
breakfast—a "meal of ceremony" at the Parker House. Dining with them
was Emma Stebbins. During the week's visit, Cushman tried to do everything she could to gain Lanier entrance into Boston's artistic circles; she
also wanted to bring attention to him in England. She invited notable
people to her rooms at the Parker House to hear Lanier play; one of these
was the American diva Clara Louise Kellogg, who recalled the evening
many years later. Lanier had played "charmingly," she wrote:

> He was poor then, and Miss Cushman was interested in him and anxious
> to help him in every way she could. . . . One composition that Lanier
> played somewhat puzzled me—my impertinent absolute pitch was, as usual,
> hard at work—and at the end I exclaimed:
> "That piece doesn't end in the same key in which it begins!"
> Lanier looked surprised and said:
> "No, it doesn't. It is one of my own compositions."
> He thought it remarkable that I could catch the change of key in such
> a long and intricately modulated piece of music.[32]

Lanier had received from Bayard Taylor notes of introduction to Henry
Wadsworth Longfellow, James Russell Lowell, and Thomas Bailey Aldrich, and Miss Cushman added her own notes to Longfellow and Lowell.[33] Lanier also requested an introduction to the actor Edwin Booth, and
Miss Cushman obliged as soon as she was able. "I am too ill to write," she
said to Booth, "and yet I made an effort to send you this word, because I
wish to present to your acquaintance what will grow to your friendship—
my dearly valued friend, Mr. Sidney Lanier." Booth would find him a man
of "great cultivation, great refinement of manner, and a knightly soul. . . .
I have made you, here, the sweetest bequest known to your true friend,

---

[31]Lanier, "To Mary Day Lanier," 2 November 1875, ibid., 266.

[32]Clara Louise Kellogg, *Memoirs of an American Prima Donna* (New York: G.
P. Putnam's Sons, 1913) 52.

[33]Lanier, "To Mary Day Lanier," 2 November 1875, CE, 9:266; Leach, *Bright
Particular Star*, 388.

Charlotte Cushman."[34] Lanier may have seen Booth later when the actor played *Richard II* in Baltimore on 14 January 1876, but there is no evidence that the two men ever actually met.[35]

Lanier did not get to meet Aldrich in Boston, but was received by Longfellow at Craigie House on 6 November; a few days later, Longfellow wrote to Taylor that he was "much pleased with Mr. Lanier." Lanier also met briefly with Lowell, who recalled a decade later that "the image of his shining presence is among the friendliest in my memory."[36] Lanier's own impressions of these meetings do not exist, but what little evidence there is suggests that not much warmth—and certainly no assistance—was generated by these encounters.[37] When this ray of hope faded, the "last resort" of the Peabody Orchestra was once more the only steady job Lanier was offered.

When Lanier left Boston, he was optimistic about Charlotte Cushman's condition. He wrote to Gibson Peacock that she was in pain, "but appears to keep up her general health steadily. I've had several talks with her doctor: —and I would not be surprised if he really cured her."[38] The physician, a Dr. Thornton, also examined Lanier. Was Lanier seeing in Miss Cushman what he wished to see, projecting his own hopes of a cure for them both? When Lanier took leave of Miss Cushman on 10 November, it was for the last time.

Several days later he was in Macon, arranging winter plans with Mary and the boys. It was resolved that, although Lanier could not support them all in Baltimore, he would take with him his eldest son, seven-year-old Charley. It would be the first real opportunity to share his artistic life with his family. The presence of his son and the comfort of his old position in the orchestra gave Lanier's life a semblance of normalcy. He thought that if only he might bring Mary and the two other boys, Sidney and Harry—named for Harry Wysham—to Baltimore, he could then be truly happy.

----

[34]Charlotte Cushman to Edwin Booth, 11 January 1876, quoted in Leach, *Bright Particular Star*, 393.

[35]CE, 9:327 n.49.

[36]Quoted in ibid., 269, notes 193, 194.

[37]Starke, *Sidney Lanier*, 220-21.

[38]Lanier, "To Gibson Peacock," 10 November 1875, CE, 9:270.

Nonetheless, December was indeed a happy month for Lanier. The concert season was going well, and the orchestra played two concerts with Hans von Bülow conducting. And Lanier, to his delight, found that although he had not been practicing, he had "wonderfully improved in tone."[39] Certainly, Asger Hamerik was happy to see Lanier again; in October, he had implored his friend: "Come, take your old place, with Wysham as your second. You can write your beautiful poetry as well in Balto as any place else."[40] Bayard Taylor came to Baltimore to deliver lectures at the Peabody Institute and enjoyed a friendly reunion with Lanier. The other boarders in the brownstone on Center Street where Lanier lived, charmed by Charley as well as his father, made the season especially festive for them.

The holidays were made even more gratifying when, on 28 December, Taylor wrote that he had named Lanier to the United States Centennial Commission, which sought a Southern poet to write a cantata for its grand exhibition to be opened in May in Philadelphia. The musical program would be conducted by Theodore Thomas, and Dudley Buck of Connecticut would write the music to Lanier's words. "Thomas remembers you well," wrote Taylor—perhaps Thomas had indeed noticed Lanier in New York, but not enough to want to help him—and "Mr. Buck says it would be specially agreeable to him to compose for the words of a Southern poet."[41] On the last day of the month, the official notice of the commission was sent to Lanier. The new year was starting well.

---

[39]Lanier, "To Mary Day Lanier," 2 December 1875, ibid., 274.

[40]Asger Hamerik to Sidney Lanier, 23 October 1875, Charles D. Lanier Papers, John Work Garrett Library, the Johns Hopkins University, Baltimore, Maryland.

[41]Bayard Taylor to Sidney Lanier, 28 December 1875, quoted in CE, 9:288-89 n.216.

CHAPTER VIII

The Centennial Cantata

IN PHILADELPHIA'S FAIRMOUNT PARK, seventy-five acres of frozen ground were being prepared for the construction of almost two hundred buildings, statues, and fountains. The land had been leveled, drained, marked into streets, and planted with utility poles since the end of 1873, but three years later only five half-finished buildings and a lot of mud were to be found on the site.[1] However, within five months, a special railroad line would link the city's center to the main entrance of the Centennial exhibition area, where broad avenues would lead hundreds of thousands of American and foreign visitors past Machinery Hall, the Women's Pavilion, Horticultural Hall, and scores of buildings representing the people and crafts of dozens of countries.

But the fair was, foremost, a showplace for America. It was the Gilded Industrial Age, and the people came to view their accomplishments, proudly strolling the park's Avenue of the Republic, past the displays of engines, model factories, a section of cable from the Brooklyn Bridge, and the telephone. For a time, at least for the six months' duration of the fair, the glories of the machine age eclipsed its abuses. What mattered most of all was that the displays were products of a united nation; at Fairmount Park, the ruling spirit was that of reconciliation.

Recognition of this spirit was also important to the fair's organizers, who, in planning the opening-day ceremonies, consciously awarded the

---

[1]William Peirce Randel, *Centennial: American Life in 1876* (New York: Chilton, 1969) 286-87.

commissions for a cantata to a Northerner and a Southerner, so that the composition itself would serve as a symbol of rededication to the Union. Lanier, who was by nature pacific and forgiving, was quick to realize the importance of the cantata's symbolism. Several days after receiving the commission, he wrote to Bayard Taylor that since the piece was to be performed "not only at our Centennial, but at a festival where the world was our invited guest, to be welcomed . . . spread-eagleism would be ungraceful and unworthy." He also formulated an aesthetic principle by which to write the words of the cantata; since "something ought to be said in the poem . . . it ought to be not rhymed philosophy, but a genuine song, and lyric outburst."[2]

In a 5 January letter, Dudley Buck told Lanier that he needed the text by 15 January and provided some guidelines. Buck and Thomas thought the cantata should have "three movements or rather one continuous movement including three episodes."[3] Buck hoped Lanier would use irregular verse, which presented no difficulty since Lanier was now doing his best work in that idiom.

But Lanier was preoccupied by his work at the Peabody, preparing a concert of Scandinavian music, as well as writing another sketch of India for *Lippincott's*, and 8 January found the cantata assignment untouched. Yet the pleasures of his musical work relieved much of the pressure now placed upon him. "In music," he wrote to Mary, "one finds an immense compensation for all the necessary repressions which come in daily life. . . . I find it growing more and more necessary to me. What will I ever do without the Orchestra?"[4] Perhaps Lanier had received inspiration from the lyricism of the pieces played that night; the concert included the Prelude to Act IV of Hamerik's opera, *Tovelille*, and the *Norse Symphony* by one of Lanier's favorites, Niels Gade. Whatever the source of inspiration, it worked; he completed the poem, at least its first draft, the next day.

Rewriting, revising, and alteration were accomplished, and on 12 January, Lanier sent Taylor another version. He included an "analysis of

---

[2]Sidney Lanier, "To Bayard Taylor," 9 January 1876, in *The Centennial Edition of the Works of Sidney Lanier*, ed. Charles R. Anderson et al., 10 vols. (Baltimore: Johns Hopkins University, 1945) 9:295 (hereafter cited as CE).

[3]Dudley Buck to Sidney Lanier, 5 January 1876, quoted in ibid., 299 n.17.

[4]Lanier, "To Mary Day Lanier," 8 January 1876, ibid., 294.

movements written in the margin."[5] He also showed the poem to Theodore Thomas, who had come to Baltimore with his orchestra for two concerts, and who was in charge of the musical program at the Centennial opening exercises; the maestro seemed quite pleased with Lanier's work.

As a musician, Lanier understood that this poem presented unique problems and realized that he "had to compose for the musician as well as the country: and had to cast the poem into such a form as would at once show well in music . . . and in poetry." He wished to make it "as large and simple as a Symphony of Beethoven's," and to this end he had to think in terms of "a kind of average and miscellaneousness" and "in *broad bands of color.*"[6] This was a concept that did not lend itself to simple explanation. As Lanier wrote the words, he continually thought of music; music suggested words to him, and these words, in turn, had to suggest notes to Buck. "I have had constantly in my mind," wrote Lanier, "those immortal melodies of Beethoven in which, with little more than the chords of the tonic and dominant, he has presented such firm, majestic, and at the same artless ideas."[7] To Lanier, the term "artless," which he used several times in his letters to Taylor and Buck, meant lacking in artifice. He wanted to present concepts as strong, free, and straightforward as the nation whose ideals they expressed. He was not interested in writing anything esoteric, too intellectual, or even "*too* original."[8] Yet, by reason of its composition according to musical concepts, the poem was quite original, and therefore provoked a range of response from admiration to open hostility.

From the first, Dudley Buck was both an enthusiastic and a sympathetic collaborator. He wrote to Lanier that he was pleased "to join partnership with a Southerner on this truly national occasion. . . . As I am so fortunate as to have a musician for my poet we shall doubtless understand each other."[9] Although the two men did not meet until the day of the cantata's performance, they found themselves to be quite compatible.

---

[5]Lanier, "To Bayard Taylor," 12 January 1876, ibid., 296.

[6]Lanier, "To Bayard Taylor," 13 January 1876, ibid., 296-97.

[7]Lanier, "To Bayard Taylor," 15 January 1876, ibid., 298.

[8]Lanier, "To Bayard Taylor," 13 January 1876, ibid., 296.

[9]Dudley Buck to Sidney Lanier, 5 January 1876, ibid., 299 n.17.

Born in Hartford in 1839, Dudley Buck graduated from Trinity College and went to Europe for the obligatory music studies. Upon returning to America, he established his reputation as a virtuoso organist, and by 1876 he was a popular composer of religious music. While in Chicago serving as organist of St. James' Episcopal Church, he suffered a devasting setback when he lost his library, including many compositions, in the Great Fire of 1871. He sought a fresh start in Boston, where he met Theordore Thomas; he became Thomas's assistant in 1875 and followed him to New York. Buck became organist and conductor of the Brooklyn Apollo Club, a position he would hold for a quarter-century. The Centennial commission established his status as a composer of cantatas; in subsequent years he wrote *Scenes from the Golden Legend* and *King Olaf's Christmas*, both based upon works by Longfellow, and *The Voyage of Columbus*, taken from the *Life of Columbus* by Washington Irving.[10] These cantatas are neglected today, if not unknown, but many of Buck's hymns are still popular.

Although Lanier wrote the poem for the cantata in a "frenzy of Creation," he spent several weeks at constant revision, often at the urging of Buck, with whom he now had "quite a voluminous correspondence."[11] They wrote almost every day—Buck making suggestions about Lanier's words with respect to their effect when pronounced by a chorus, and Lanier responding favorably to Buck's notes. Lanier had originally titled his work the *Centennial Song of Columbia* until Buck had asked him if this was really the most appropriate title. "The word 'Song' seems to me hardly worthy of the calibre of the poem. . . . It occurred to me that perhaps, on second thoughts, you might prefer Centennial Musings or Meditations (or the like)—of Columbia."[12] Lanier thanked him for this idea and happily adopted it. With all matters regarding the text smoothed and settled, Buck proceeded with his monumental task—setting the challenging poem to music and scoring it for performance by a 150-piece orchestra and a chorus of 800. He was aided in this by Lanier's suggestive annotations in the mar-

---

[10]Gilbert Chase, *America's Music: From the Pilgrims to the Present*, rev. 2d ed. (New York: McGraw-Hill, 1966) 334-35; CE, 9:292-93 n.5.

[11]Lanier, "To Mary Day Lanier," 22 January 1876, CE, 9:305.

[12]Dudley Buck to Sidney Lanier, 30 January 1876, ibid., 312 n.33.

gins of the text; the opening chorus should be written with "sober, measured and yet majestic progressions of chords" and a "quartette" section should be in "a meagre and despairing minor."[13]

Both Buck and Lanier were excited by the project and were optimistic of its success at the exhibition's opening ceremonies in May. However, it was not Lanier's fate to have even one undisturbed success. Against his strong objections, the text of the cantata was released to the press before the scheduled premiere. Lanier knew that the words were only part of a whole and could not be fairly judged without the music. Publication of the text without benefit of music made as much sense as publishing an opera libretto and calling it a poem. Lanier, Thomas, and Buck understood that the cantata had to be appreciated as the union of artistic purpose it was designed to be—the cumulative creation of poet, composer, conductor, chorus, and orchestra.

But New York *Tribune* music critic J. R. G. Hassard did not understand this, and on 31 March he opened the barrage of criticism that Lanier feared pre-performance publication would start. Hassard received a piano-vocal score of the cantata from its publisher, G. Schirmer of New York; he praised the music but called Lanier's text "sometimes obscure" and found at least one passage a "tough morsel."[14] Bayard Taylor, after speaking with Hassard, was reassured that no malice was meant toward Lanier and tried to calm the poet. But Lanier, knowing that "many of the people who will read this Tribune attack are not only incapable of judging its correctness but will be prevented from seeing the whole poem for yet six weeks,"[15] framed a letter of defense. Taylor, ever the voice of moderation, urged him not to send it.

This was the beginning of a bitter time for Lanier, though friends like Buck and Taylor defended him ardently. Buck wrote that the "pitfalls"— using Hassard's word—which the poetry presented to the composer "were rather godsends."[16] Taylor spoke to fellow clubman Whitelaw Reid, edi-

---

[13]*The Centennial Meditation of Columbia*, CE, 1:60-62.

[14]Aubrey Harrison Starke, *Sidney Lanier: A Biographical and Critical Study* (reprint, New York: Russell and Russell, 1964) 240.

[15]Lanier, "To Bayard Taylor," 1 April 1876, CE, 9:349.

[16]Dudley Buck to Sidney Lanier, 4 April 1876, quoted in ibid., 354-55 n.83.

tor of the *Tribune*, and arranged to have the full text of the cantata published in the paper, with "an appropriate and explanatory introduction"
written by Taylor himself. In it, he would do his best to "set other papers
upon the track of a right understanding."[17] The poem, with Taylor's introduction, was printed on 12 April. Lanier's work, noted Taylor, had
"greater freedom and freshness" than that written by Tennyson for the International Exhibition in London.

Nonetheless, the attacks continued. In its 13 April issue, the *Nation*
claimed that Lanier's poem was perhaps "suitable to a commemoration of
the Declaration of Independence, as it is a practical assertion of emanci-
pation from the ordinary laws of sense and sound, melody and prosody.
. . . But that the music is already composed for it, we should hope it was
not too late to save American letters from the humiliation of presenting
to the world such a farrago as this as their choicest product."[18]

Southern newspapers, as well as those of Baltimore and Philadelphia,
rallied to defend Lanier against invectives such as this. The Baltimore
Bulletin printed the poem, and its critic (possibly Lanier's friend, writer
Innes Randolph) stated that the poetry for a cantata "must lie on the bor-
derland between thought and melody; and it is in that region that Mr. Lanier is most happy and at home . . . himself a musician, and keenly alive
to musical 'motives' as well as poetic thoughts."[19]

It was unfortunate that the cantata, a symbol of reconciliation, was
itself becoming a controversy with regional overtones. But it was hoped
that the actual performance would win approval during the jubilation of
the opening ceremonies. Surely Lanier would be vindicated then.

The morning of 10 May 1876 promised rain, but a quarter of a million
people ignored the skies, determined to attend the opening of the American Centennial Exhibition. The crowd that awaited the beginning of the
ceremonies at ten o'clock was so huge, wrote a reporter for the *New York
Times*, that he could not even compute it; the crowd "was simply enor-

[17]Bayard Taylor to Sidney Lanier, 11 April 1876, quoted in ibid., 355 n.85.

[18]Quoted in ibid., 360 n.89.

[19]Baltimore *Bulletin*, 15 April 1876, quoted in ibid., 361 n.89.

mous and fainting men were dragged out by the Police by the dozens."[20] A contemporary engraving depicting the scene at the plaza area shows every bit of space—in front of the reviewing stand and the musicians' platforms, around the flagpoles and equestrian statues—packed with spectators, many carrying umbrellas.

When the American flag atop the main building was unfurled, wrote an observer, "every other flag was opened to the breeze, the chimes began a joyful peal, and the grand Hallelujah chorus of Handel, performed by one thousand singers, and full orchestral and organ accompaniment, gave fitting expression to the popular joy."[21] As the orchestra, led by Theodore Thomas, played various national anthems, thousands passed through the gates and massed before the reviewing stands where dignitaries including President Ulysses S. Grant and Dom Pedro II, emperor of Brazil, were assembled. The program began with the *Centennial Inauguration March* by Richard Wagner; whereas the commission of this work indicates the level of popularity Wagner had reached in America by 1876, this piece was one of his most disappointing. The *Centennial Hymn*, with music by John Knowles Paine and words by John Greenleaf Whittier, followed. But "the conspicuous feature of all,"[22] stated the Baltimore *Sun*, was the cantata. This work, reported the *New York Times*, "afforded [the] most satisfaction. . . . unquestionably the most successful effort of the day."[23]

The *Centennial Meditation of Columbia* was a triumph. Lanier sat proudly in the reviewing stand as Buck led the huge chorus and orchestra in the exciting performance. The influence of the work upon the massed audience, wrote the *Times*, was "more decisive than either the hymn or Wagner's march." The solo passage of the "Good Angel," sung by basso Myron Whitney of Boston, had to be repeated because "the enthusiasm of the auditors took the shape of a recall, and Mr. Buck had to appear and acknowledge a liberal tribute of applause."[24] The Baltimore *Sun* wrote that

---

[20]*New York Times*, 11 May 1876, 1.

[21]C. B. Taylor, *One Hundred Years' Achievements of a Free People* (New York: Henry S. Allen, 1876) 718.

[22]Baltimore *Sun*, 11 May 1876, 1.

[23]*New York Times*, 11 May 1876, 1.

[24]Ibid., 2.

Whitney's "lowest notes were like the tremulous vibration of an organ's pipes, causing the excited listeners . . . to exclaim 'Superb!' 'Bravo!' and to declare that it was the best thing of the hour."[25]

Unfortunately, no contemporary account records any special tribute paid to Lanier, but he was exhilarated nonetheless and wrote to his father: "I wish I had time to give you some idea *how* great it was; probably nothing like it has ever been beheld or heard." The bass solo, he wrote, "was heard by at least twenty five thousand people, and was encored,—both of which circumstances are probably without parallel on an occasion of this kind."[26] Lanier's comments were not the result of egotism but of joy at seeing his dream—musical poetry wedded to poetic music—fulfilled, and having its realization received with admiration and appreciation. This cantata was the culmination of a total aesthetic experience in which lyrics were not, as Lanier put it, "a rhymed set of good adages," but were, with the music, mutually suggestive of the ideas presented; it was a pioneer effort in American artistic creation.

That evening Lanier and Buck attended a reception with President Grant and Dom Pedro, Lanier thoroughly enjoying the excitement of which he was a part. But his happiness was spoiled the next day—as many days and weeks would continue to be marred—by the continuation of criticism heaped upon his poetry. "Many of the papers," he wrote sadly to Mary, "have renewed the most bitter abuse and ridicule upon my poor little Cantata, and have displayed an amount of gratuitous cruelty and ignorant brutality of which I could never have dreamed."[27] To Lanier, who probably never had a malicious thought, who was rarely angry and always forgiving, this was crushing.

Despite the acclaim of the audience and the support of the Philadelphia and Baltimore newspapers, other critics, notably in New York, continued to disparage Lanier. There was one positive account in the New York *Tribune*—written by Bayard Taylor. "I wish some of the critics who were made so unhappy by Mr. Lanier's cantata could have heard it sung. . . . It was original in the perfection of the execution no less than in the

---

[25]Baltimore *Sun*, 11 May 1876, 1.

[26]Lanier, "To Robert S. Lanier," 12 May 1876, CE, 9:363.

[27]Lanier, "To Mary Day Lanier," 2 June 1876, ibid., 364.

conception of both poet and composer. The effect upon the audience could not be mistaken."[28] And in an editorial in his *Bulletin*, Gibson Peacock stated that Lanier, "with all the stirring of original conception alive within him, could not dare to be anything on such an occasion that was not wholly true to his own genius, his own idea of art."[29] The *Philadelphia New Century For Women* declared that the cantata was "the century itself, two centuries in its bosom. Those who have not heard it sung, have not begun to spell its meaning."[30]

Though these comments pleased Lanier, he was more affected by such as those appearing in the New York *Herald*: "Mr. Lanier . . . has written a beautiful poem, but it is obscure to the eye and must be unintelligible to the ear. . . . The argument of the poem is not easily to be comprehended, and the language is harsh." An editorial in the *New York Times* called the cantata a "bewildering collection of rhymes . . . entirely at variance with the taste of the American people."[31] At least two parodies of Lanier's words also appeared. This was too much for Lanier's normally stoic nature. "How bitter," he cried to Mary, "is the heedless hurt of this hoofed Stupidity which one cannot allow himself to hate!" Neither did he want the poem to be acclaimed by people simply because they admired him personally; he wanted them to understand the purpose of his art. But his friends, he said, "do not know what I am about, and the cheap triumph of wrong praise is but a pain to the Artist."[32] He decided to send his letter of explanation and defense to the New York *Tribune*, the one Bayard Taylor had urged him not to send.

The letter explained his philosophy of musical verse and the special problems of a poet writing words to be sung: sound had to express ideas just as effectively as words; only general conceptions could be depicted; the words had to be ones easily enunciated by the chorus; and sectional movements had to have clear delineations in sound. Lanier's thesis was that major changes had to be made "in the relations of Poetry to Music by

[28]Quoted in ibid., 363 n.91.

[29]Quoted in ibid., 366 n.97.

[30]Ibid.

[31]Quoted in ibid., 364 n.94.

[32]Lanier, "To Mary Day Lanier," 15 May 1876, ibid., 365-66.

the prodigious modern development of the orchestra."[33] Revealing his familiarity with Schubert, Beethoven, Berlioz, Liszt, Saint-Saëns, Meyerbeer, and Rossini, he traced the progress of orchestral technique—and therefore complexity of structure in composition—in their musical expression. But he was chiefly impressed by Wagner's ability to express intellectual conceptions through the use of instrumentation, and this admiration for Wagner's manipulation of musical textures is ultimately reflected in Lanier's own manipulation of verbal texture. The essay is a cogent explanation of the effects of programme music upon Lanier's poetry and how his poetry was constructed with musical principles in mind.

However, this letter had no effect upon those who had desired merely a pretty poem for their centennial. It did serve to continue the controversy. And, unfortunately, it finally exposed Lanier's long-repressed anger, anger at the "endeavor of certain newspapers to belittle the largest anniversary's celebration of our country by the treatment of one of its constituent features" without any attempt to understand it, and the display of "inexcusable disregard for the proprieties of a dignified occasion and for the laws of respectable behavior."[34]

Dwight's Journal of Music, as the chief monitor of American musical life, had been following the conflict closely. In its issue of 27 May 1876, it reprinted the text of the cantata (as well as that of Whittier's hymn), followed by a reprint of Lanier's letter to the *Tribune* on 10 June. Two weeks later the journal printed an unsigned article entitled "A New Sydney's 'Defense' of a New Kind 'of Poesy.' " The author of this article called the Centennial cantata the "strangest and the last result of Wagnerism! . . . [Lanier], who is also a musician, member of an orchestra of ultra-modern tendencies—has eaten of the insane root, and has become intensely Wagnerized." Stating that he too understood that poetry and music could be wed, the critic believed that had already been accomplished best by Bach in his cantatas. But Wagner had changed all this, stressing drama and orchestral expression, so that the voice "simply interprets, calls the names, points with a stick . . . we should hardly miss the singing." And Lanier's cantata, following "this modern striving after novelty," suffered a loss in clarity. Interestingly, the author of this critique does not so much dis-

---

[33]"The Centennial Cantata," CE, 2:266.

[34]Ibid., 273.

credit Lanier, whose *The Symphony* he admired and whose general purposes he understood. The villain of the whole drama, according to the critic, was Wagner, for the "stupendous overshadowing modern orchestra, with the vast revolutionary Wagner phantom behind it, has disturbed Lanier's poetic spontaneity and spoiled his poem. . . . a theoretic bugbear intervened to make the verbal expression purposely obscure."[35] The development of modern music and of the orchestra, which Lanier credited as an aid to the development of his poetry, was labeled here a corrupting influence.

Two weeks later, continuing to monitor the controversy, *Dwight's* carried yet another article, reprinted from the July issue of the *Atlantic Monthly*—never any friend to Lanier and certainly not one now. The *Atlantic's* critic, W. F. Apthorp, found that "Mr. Buck has been unfortunate in the text to which he has written music." Lanier's poem, the article stated, might be "suitable to musical treatment in the dramatic, declamatory Liszt-Wagner style, but is very ill adapted to musical treatment in the purely musical style in which Mr. Buck is so gracefully at home." Apparently the *Atlantic* wished composers to be as genteel as the writers of whom it approved, for it found Buck's work so "capital," and "so pure and unforced," that it could "overlook an occasional tendency to the trivial and commonplace." It could forgive Buck's conservatism—for, in truth, he was no pioneer of creativity—but not Lanier's innovation. Lanier, "in expounding the alphabet of a new poetic-musical art . . . has forgotten that it must have a grammar also."[36]

It is sad that, whereas Lanier did enjoy acclaim as the honored Centennial poet, so many writers and publications saw fit to tear him limb from limb for his efforts. Yet there are grounds for many legitimate and unprejudiced criticisms. Buck's music was more easily comprehended in 1876 than was Lanier's poetry, and therefore was dealt with gently at the time—but it cannot be spared from an examination that finds it less than satisfactory. If the *Centennial Meditation of Columbia* is not an entirely gratifying work, it is because of a certain awkwardness in both poetry and music.

Those critics who lambasted Lanier's poem could not understand his concept of depicting the various forces molding the American nation as

---

[35]*Dwight's Journal of Music* (24 June 1876): 255.

[36]"The Centennial Cantata," *Dwight's Journal of Music* (8 July 1876): 261.

contrasting "broad bands" of sound. Some contemporary commentators, however, such as the reporter for the *New Century For Women*, did comprehend and endeavored to impress their appreciation upon their readers. The reporter for the *New York Times* who attended the ceremonies understood; while he criticized the music, he found in it those qualities which proved how well Buck had attempted to adhere to Lanier's ideals. "The merits of the score are perhaps somewhat unequal, and the themes are not always of marked excellence, but the cantata is full of variety of rhythm and tempo, and replete with contrast."[37] Another defense of Lanier came from C. B. Taylor, author of an 1876 history of the United States, the narrative of which culminates in a description of the centennial exhibition. He noted that "in reading the lines we must remember the musical restrictions under which Mr. Lanier was held. Within the compass of sixty lines he was obliged to make direct reference to the changes, contrasts, and combinations of voices and instruments. None but a musician as well as a poet could have done this, and it was Mr. Lanier's proficiency in both arts which enabled him to attain his present success."[38]

In many ways the *Centennial Meditation of Columbia* resembles *The Symphony*, for similar ideas and vehicles are used. The cantata is divided into several distinct sections, and the controlling sense-image is sound—it is the history of the United States in timbre and tone. Accordingly, Buck had to complement each section with its own appropriate musical setting, but still provide unity so the piece would not have a choppy effect. This was no simple task, especially considering what Buck called "this miserable writing against time." Although both poet and composer worked valiantly, the results, to some extent, prove that creativity could be inspired, but not upon demand.

In the cantata, Columbia, seated upon her vantage point of a "hundred-terraced height," reflects upon her past and listened as "old voices rise and call" from her history. Buck attempted to give the "voices"—those of early settlers, the elements of nature they fought, the sounds of war—individual characterizations, but he achieved only partial success. As much in

---

[37]*New York Times*, 11 May 1876, 1.

[38]Taylor, *One Hundred Years' Achievements*, 723.

agreement with each other as Lanier and Buck may have been, they were not totally well suited.

The basic problem stemmed from Lanier being an unconventional poet—though many of his works are in traditional form, his more ambitious works belong to what was then the avant-garde—and Buck being a conventional composer whose creations never became the subject of public debate. Buck, as Gilbert Chase notes, "wrote for the taste of the day and for a ready market."[39] He was a European-trained American composer of the imitative school, which is evident in the cantata. At times the music is like that of a traditional hymn, while other sections have echoes of Beethoven and Verdi; whereas a variety of stylistic expression might have been what Lanier wanted, the aesthetic results, musically, are less than outstanding because they contain nothing unique, and very little of the music is memorable. The *Atlantic Monthly* was correct in saying that "Mr. Buck does not write with a very Titanic pen,"[40] but it found less fault with his musical understatement than with Lanier's more daring efforts. The "merely general" in music was more acceptable to a conservative audience than generalized concepts expressed in verse.

While sympathetic to Lanier's ideas, Buck was simply not predisposed to writing music much different from his previous works or from other popular works in the current mode; his training negated it. The writer for *Dwight's Journal of Music* saw this, realizing that although Buck's music "is perfectly clear as music (and very clever too in many parts) . . . it does not help at all to make the enigmatical lines of the poem any clearer. No, this music quietly takes them on its back and flows on at 'its own sweet will,' unconscious of the burden." The author remarks that, given lines such as:

> *Yonder where the to-and-fro*
> *Weltering of my Long-Ago*
> *Moves about the moveless base*
> *Far below my resting place*
> (ll. 7-10)

Buck makes "no particular ado" in setting them to music. Here was "a chance to 'welter,' too, after the approved Wagner fashion; but our com-

---

[39]Chase, *America's Music*, 335.

[40]*Dwight's Journal of Music* (8 July 1876): 261.

poser, bound before all things to write musically and clearly, is not tempted."[41] Most likely this was meant as praise, faint as it may sound, but with a tone of subtle irony that hints of disapproval of Buck's lack of adventurousness. But how could Buck have written otherwise? He had an established mode of composition; his traditional, conventional music could not have been an equal partner to experimental verse. Therefore, the four lines quoted above, rather than rolling and surging as the words suggest, are delivered in the lovely but predictable harmonies of a hymn. Lanier had asked that this first section be given "sober, measured and yet majestic progressions of chords,"[42] and this is just what Buck provided, in the only mode he knew.

As long as Lanier's words remained on a concrete level, Buck had little trouble working with them. The second section, depicting the Mayflower "Trembling westward o'er yon balking sea" (l. 12), with the sighs of the Pilgrims in conflict with the shouting of "Gray-lipp'd waves" (l. 15), is provided with effective, if rather trite, "storm music." But when Lanier moves to the abstract level, difficulties begin for both composer and audience. Here it is possible to understand the criticism that Lanier's poem was vague:

> Then old Shapes and Masks of Things,
> Framed like Faiths or clothed like Kings—
> Ghosts of Goods once fleshed and fair,
> Grown foul Bads in alien air—
> (ll. 23-26)

These lines introduce the theme of war, an idea not difficult to render through music. However, the more abstract concepts were much more problematic to communicate. The combination of this difficulty and the realization that these lines are far from Lanier's best validates some of the criticism. There are also others that would prompt negative criticism: "Toil through the stertorous death of the Night" (l. 41), or "Jamestown, out of thee— / Plymouth, thee—thee, Albany" (ll. 17-18). And any reader familiar with poems that described things exactly, or with identifiable im-

---

[41]"A New Sydney's 'Defense' of a New Kind 'of Poesy,' " *Dwight's Journal of Music* (24 June 1876): 255.

[42]Marginal annotation to lines 1-10, CE, 2:60.

agery, would certainly stop at "Yonder where the to-and-fro / Weltering of my Long-Ago" and would wonder how a "Long-Ago" weltered.

There are lines and sections, however, where Lanier is majestic, and although Buck tries to meet him, he falls short. Lanier may have had the "immortal melodies of Beethoven" in mind while he wrote his words, but unfortunately he was not working with a Beethoven. When Lanier's words are bad, Buck's music is mediocre; when Lanier's words are excellent, Buck's music is merely good.

The finest part of the cantata comes at the end, when Columbia declares in triumph—"Despite the land, despite the sea, / I was: I am: and I shall be" (ll. 46-47)—but wishes the "Good Angel" to tell her how long the republic can expect to last. The answer—the basso solo encored by the audience—contains six conditions which, if met, will ensure the permanence of America. These few lines are masterpieces of richness, terse and yet full:

> *"Long as thine Art shall love true love,*
> *Long as thy Science truth shall know,*
> *Long as thine Eagle harms no Dove,*
> *Long as thy Law by law shall grow,*
> *Long as thy God is God above,*
> *Thy brother every man below,*
> *So long, dear Land of all my love,*
> *Thy name shall shine, thy fame shall glow!"*
> (ll. 50-57)

This is the closest that Lanier comes to writing a "rhymed set of good adages." But here this parallel set of simple and straightforward maxims, easy to deliver and to comprehend, is most appropriate.

In the final chorus, music is proclaimed to be the herald of a harmonious future:

> *O Music, from this height of time my Word unfold:*
> *In thy large signals all men's hearts thy Heart behold*
> (ll. 58-59)

These lines are given the majestic, hymn-like theme of the opening of the cantata, but unfortunately the next couplet, the concluding lines, is rendered virtually indistinguishable. The composer, self-consciously aware that he was writing a Buck cantata, decided to introduce a great fugue. Fugal singing renders the words difficult to understand under the best of conditions, and outdoor delivery by a chorus of eight hundred must have been thunderously chaotic. A fugue was certainly not the easiest method of presenting these lines of, as Lanier annotated them, "jubilation and welcome":

> Mid-heaven unroll thy chords as friendly flags unfurled,
> And wave the world's best lover's welcome to the world.

The controversy over the centennial cantata lasted long after its concluding brass and percussion fanfares had died away. But being controversial was preferable to being unknown. Lanier's words were read by tens of thousands who never heard Buck's music. The cantata was performed again in the fall of 1876 at Theodore Thomas's Centennial Musical Festival, and then the music was packed off to obscurity. Today, Lanier's poem can be found in his collected works in any major library, but the piano-vocal score published by Schirmer is a rarity; Dudley Buck's original score and orchestral parts remain in manuscript, wrapped in brown paper and tied with string.

The opening day of the Centennial Exhibition was, for Sidney Lanier, a day of celebration and a time for putting to public test his idea of musical-poetic unity. In some ways his efforts were still rough and tentative, but judging from the cheers of the three hundred thousand people who heard the cantata performed, he was a success. And from the turmoil generated by his words, it was evident that Lanier was a literary figure who could not be ignored.

CHAPTER IX

1876:
In Search of a Word

THE CENTENNIAL CANTATA had not consumed all of Lanier's time during the spring of 1876, although it was the project with which he was most obsessed. There were numerous other matters that pressed for his attention, including the demands of the orchestra and other musical engagements, the "India" assignments from *Lippincott's*, rewriting an article on the "Physics of Music," and, increasingly, poetry. Almost as soon as he had finished writing the poem for the cantata, he began work on a "Centennial poem" commissioned by *Lippincott's* to appear in its July issue.

However, Lanier was so fatigued that he wished he might have a respite from writing, both to "refresh a much-worn physique" and to prepare his thoughts. He also wanted "to read many things which are of necessity to me in both my arts."[1] A letter to poet Edward Spencer reveals how this reading reflected his own interests in synaesthesia. A line from Shakespeare's Sonnet 23—"To hear with eyes belongs to Love's fine wit."— seemed "completely a nutshell judgment on my side as regards the possibility of interpreting . . . one sense by another through the form of art." Lanier found that this description fit what he was trying to do in *The Symphony*. He told Spencer that he had found one of the *Florentine Nights* of Heinrich Heine "doing exactly what the Symphony does, *i.e.* interpreting

---

[1]Sidney Lanier, "To Mary Day Lanier," 13 February 1876, in *The Centennial Edition of the Works of Sidney Lanier*, ed. Charles R. Anderson et al., 10 vols. (Baltimore: Johns Hopkins Press, 1945) 9:321 (hereafter cited as CE).

a musical work through the form of a vision." Although this translation of Heine had been published in New York in 1873, Lanier did not see it "until long after 'The Symphony' was written."[2]

Lanier had been influenced by other artists concerned with a union of the arts, but now he was thinking and working independently. He had gained significant confidence and skill since the publication of *Corn* in February 1875, and now he happily wrote to Mary: "How much I have been granted by the good God of the success an artist loves, in that time, and what immense strides I have made within my heart beyond the artistic crudeness and babyhood of this same February a year ago!"[3] In this feeling of optimism and confidence, Lanier began work on *Psalm of the West.*

He now found *Lippincott's* happy to take many of his poems and had arranged for the March issue to carry his sonnet "To Charlotte Cushman." Miss Cushman, he wrote to Mary on 16 February, "does not know I have sent the poem to the printer, and it will be a pleasant surprise to her."[4] Surely she would have been flattered by Lanier's tender compliments, calling her "a three-point star . . . Art's artist, Love's dear woman, Fame's good queen!"[5]

But Charlotte Cushman never saw this tribute; she died on 18 February. Three days later Lanier journeyed to Boston for her funeral where Emma Stebbins gave him a ring that Miss Cushman had wanted him to have, an antique jacinth ring carved with the masks of comedy and tragedy. The death of Charlotte Cushman affected Lanier deeply, for she had been one of the few people who had truly understood him and had championed his ideals. A week later, Lanier wrote to Bayard Taylor: "It has been up-hill work with me to struggle against the sense of loss which the departure of my beloved Charlotte Cushman leaves me. She and you were

---

[2]Lanier, "To Edward Spencer," 12 February 1876, ibid., 319. Lanier is probably referring to the *First Night,* which describes, with much emphasis upon sense, Paganini giving a concert. *Prose and Poetry by Heinrich Heine,* ed. and introd. Ernest Rhys (New York: E. P. Dutton, 1934) 272-79.

[3]Lanier, "To Mary Day Lanier," 13 February 1876, CE, 9:321.

[4]Lanier, "To Mary Day Lanier," 16 February 1876, ibid., 323.

[5]Lanier, "To Charlotte Cushman," CE, 1:58.

the only friends among the Artists I have ever had: and since she is gone I am as one who has lost the half of his possessions."[6]

The beginning of March found Lanier sorely missing his family, although Charley was still with him, and Lanier's contracting a cold only worsened his moroseness. When the cold continued until he became very ill, his characteristic optimism was replaced by doubt. He wrote to Taylor that he had been confined to a sickbed for a week, "a week whose place in the General Plan of Good I find as much difficulty in justifying as croton-bugs or children born idiots or the sausage-grinding School of poetry."[7] But he was back to his tasks as soon as he was able, trying to complete the *Psalm of the West* by April so it could be prepared for illustration and typesetting.

The poem was complete by 4 April; it was, Lanier noted, his longest poem, covering forty-one pages of manuscript paper. "It has been a sheer matter of inspiration. . . . I have found myself presently rapt away into a Heaven of Inventions where all the artistic principles which I wish to infuse into the old veins of poetry lay clearly defined before me."[8] This poem, writes Aubrey Starke, was one which, "in accordance with his maturing poetic theories," could "carry or create its own musical accompaniment."[9] Lanier actually hoped to set this work to music, for in a list of plans he outlined in an 1881 letter he mentioned hoping to write a "*Choral Symphony*, for chorus and Orchestra, being my *Psalm of the West*, with music."[10] But if any of this music was ever written, it has not been found.

Psalm of the West appeared in the July issue of *Lippincott's*—without illustrations—filling fourteen pages of the magazine, and paid Lanier a much-needed $300. The Philadelphia *Evening Bulletin* carried an editorial—presumably written by the obliging Gibson Peacock—on 23 June, praising this and other works of Lanier.

---

[6]Lanier, "To Bayard Taylor," 27 February 1876, CE, 9:328. Lanier would also outlive Taylor, who died in 1878.

[7]Lanier, "To Bayard Taylor," 11 March 1876, ibid., 332.

[8]Lanier, "To Mary Day Lanier," 4 April 1876, ibid., 350 n.81.

[9]Aubrey Harrison Starke, *Sidney Lanier: A Biographical and Critical Study* (reprint, New York: Russell and Russell, 1964) 248.

[10]Lanier, "To Sarah J. Farley," 12 February 1881, CE, 10:290.

Whatever the small-fry critics of the day may say, there can be no doubt that the most individual and national of all American poets is Mr. Sidney Lanier. . . . The "Psalm of the West" is the boldest and most successful effort ever made to put into literature, of the grand, heroic kind, the prosaic story of the discovery of America and the building up of the free Republic of the United States. . . . Lanier has devised forms of verse, of rhythm and of rhyme, which, without violating the accepted rules of standard English versification, show the resources of our language in a richness that has not before been displayed. . . . We have a right to claim for him the very first position among young American poets; perhaps that of the founder of a new and great school of English poetry created on American soil.[11]

These words appeared in the midst of the controversy over the Centennial cantata and must have been a balm to Lanier's spirit.

This criticism is competent, if also extravagant. The poem does effectively utilize various metrical forms—Gay Wilson Allen notes that there are eighteen[12]—that create contrast and a feeling of motion. Written while the idea of the Centennial cantata still dominated Lanier's mind, the Psalm is itself a cantata, with different sections suggesting treatment as recitative, aria, or chorus. The long metrical lines describing the spiraling flight of the artist, the "all-lover" who is presented with the unfolding pageant of America, suggest the narrative technique of the recitative. The more lyrical description of the Norsemen's journey is set in the mode of an aria; and the terse, compact, and stately sections, such as the concluding stanzas, are fit for choral treatment. No record exists, however, of exactly what Lanier had as a musical plan, there being nothing like the annotation for the centennial cantata with which he provided Buck.

The musical nature of the Psalm is suggested early in the poem, with the introduction of the artist. This can only be Lanier himself, for he is described with an image that Lanier had used in a letter the year before:[13]

[11]"Sidney Lanier's New Poem," (Philadelphia) Evening Bulletin, 23 June 1876, 4.

[12]American Prosody (New York: American Book Company, 1935) 291.

[13]Lanier, "To Gibson Peacock," 31 July 1875, CE, 9:224.

And ever Time tossed him bitterly to and fro
As a shuttle inlaying a perilous warp of woe
In the woof of things from terminal snow to snow. [14]

But the past and future, approaching as the wings of the East and West, raise this soul; his song then carries him up to God, who presents the panorama of history. The lines depicting the artist's song are among the most synaesthetic in the entire work:

And the uttering of song was like to the giving of light;
And he learned that hearing and seeing wrought nothing alone,
And that music on earth much light upon Heaven had thrown,
And he melted-in silvery sunshine with silvery tone;
And the spirals of music e'er higher and higher he wound
Till the luminous cinctures of melody up from the ground
Arose as the shaft of a tapering tower of sound—
(CE, 1:64)

Not all of the *Psalm* is as lucidly effective as this; many lines are strained, with awkward inversions and the heaviness of Lanier's biblicomedieval syntax: "Her shalt thou clasp for a balm to the scars of thy breast" (CE, 1:62); "Now haste thee while the way is clear, / Paul Revere! / Haste, Dawes! but haste thou not, O Sun! / To Lexington" (CE, 1:74). In fact, Lanier tries to cram too much into the *Psalm*, both historically—the explorations of the Vikings and Columbus, the American Revolution, the Civil War, and the promise of Manifest Destiny—and metrically—an exploration of the possibilities of language-exploitation. In parts it gluts the ears; the poet John Gould Fletcher found it "shot through and through" with abstractions ("And Art be known as the soul making love to the All"—similar to those abstractions for which Lanier was criticized in the Centennial cantata), and went on to call it a "monument of misplaced ingenuity . . . very nearly unreadable."[15] Here, as in the Centennial cantata, Lanier's ambitions and ideas were ahead of his practice.

In a poem of this length (this was to remain Lanier's longest poem), there undoubtedly will be some inconsistency in quality. Parts are good; even a couplet will occasionally strike a strong chord:

---

[14]*Psalm of the West*, CE, 1:62-82. This reference is to lines 46-48.

[15]"Sidney Lanier," *The University of Kansas City Review* 16 (Winter 1949): 100.

O manful tongue, to work and sing,
And soothe a child and dare a king!
(CE, 1:81)

The variation in metrical form is sometimes artificial—for instance, introducing his early (1865) ballad-like poem, *The Tournament: Joust First,* as a treatment of the Civil War. Another early poem, *June Dreams, in January* (1868, revised 1873), appears as the hymn of the "Spirits of June-Heat." But these inclusions of earlier style are nicely contrasted with Lanier's new free-flowing longer lines; the sense of sweep they create is often enhanced by incantorial repetition. Here Lanier is anticipating Whitman's "lists" and "catalogues"; but he did not read Whitman until two years later, in 1878.

As an experiment in verse, *Psalm of the West* is successful, although it is also ponderous and imperfect. Its operatic sweep and occasional grandeur—"Land of the willful gospel . . . Tall Adam of lands" (CE, 1:62)—indicate the promise of more polished works to come. It symbolically combines Lanier's early and mature poetry, his little arias and masterful recitatives, preparing the way for his completely new poetry—the musical meditations that would appear within the next few years.

When the summer of 1876 arrived the Peabody season ended, most of the commotion over the Centennial cantata subsided, and Lanier was once again working at his independent projects. Emma Stebbins elicited Lanier's help in writing a biography of Charlotte Cushman; the book would be published by Osgood and Company of Boston. At the end of June, Lanier journeyed to Boston to make the arrangements with Osgood, who gave him the first of four monthly payments of $250. Unfortunately, Emma Stebbins was in poor health, and the project was postponed; Lanier had to return the money. The next winter, Miss Stebbins wrote to tell Lanier that the idea would have to be abandoned.[16] In the interlude, Lanier sent four poems to Dudley Buck, who wanted to set them to music. It is not certain which poems Lanier sent, but Buck returned them in August, finding them unsuitable for musical setting. However, Buck did write a setting for *Evening Song.* Lanier also renewed his efforts of securing a place in scholarly circles, requesting from a relative an introduction to Daniel

---

[16]Starke, *Sidney Lanier,* 266.

Coit Gilman,[17] president of the Johns Hopkins University, which was to open in Baltimore in September. This began Lanier's two-year battle for academic recognition.

Lanier finally realized one of his dreams that summer—he was joined by Mary and the three boys, and they lived on a farm in West Chester, Pennsylvania, a few miles from Philadelphia. The domestic tranquility eased Lanier's disappointments over the uncertainty of his career. But he was also quite ill, his condition undoubtedly aggravated by the many strains under which he had been placed during the year; from this summer his illness attacked him with increasing severity. Aubrey Starke points out that, to the consumptive, disappointments "are fatal, and that summer disappointments came to Lanier in rapid succession."[18] His poems were rejected, the plan for the Cushman biography dissolved, and a tentative hope of playing in Thomas's orchestra was again destroyed.

The months at West Chester should have been spent in total rest, but that was something Lanier could not do. He prepared a small volume of collected poems, which the firm of J. B. Lippincott and Company planned to publish. He wrote two essays that he hoped to sell: "The Orchestra of To-Day" was accepted by *Scribner's Monthly* in November, but was not published until 1880; and "From Bacon to Beethoven" finally appeared in *Lippincott's* seven years after Lanier's death.

The first essay is a guide to the instruments of the orchestra, enlivened by Lanier's comments on various symphonic works, emotional outbursts about music—"can any one attend . . . to an intelligent rendition of the Fifth Symphony without finding beneath all its surface-ideas this same powerful current of Desire which sets the soul insensibly closer toward the unknown by methods which are inarticulate and vague"[19]—and prophecies on the future of the orchestra. Some of his most remarkable comments concern the opportunities for women in the symphonic orchestra; Lanier, in his desire to see the joys of music shared by all, sees no reason why women should not play any instrument, except for the double-bass and heavy brass. "There is no limit," he cries, "to the possible achieve-

---

[17]Lanier, "To Robert S. Lanier," 24 July 1876, CE, 9:389.

[18]Starke, *Sidney Lanier*, 259.

[19]CE, 2:292.

ments of our countrywomen in this behalf. . . . Let our young ladies . . . address themselves to the violin, the flute, the oboe, the harp, the clarinet, the bassoon, the kettledrum. It is more than possible that upon some of these instruments the superior daintiness of the female tissue might finally make the woman a more successful player than the man."[20] This quaint combination of tender chivalry and odd progressivism apparently had no effect upon the personnel managers of nineteenth-century American orchestras.

"From Bacon to Beethoven" is a tribute to music as the "characteristic art-form of the modern time," a mixture of insight—a defense of the phenomenon of programme music—and fallacious statements born of emotion rather than scholarship. "Freed from the stern exactions of the intellect, [music] is also freed from the terrible responsibilities of realism."[21] His Puritan strain emerges in an equation of art and morality; the "consummate masters of the art"—Palestrina, Bach, and Beethoven—had nothing to do with "sheriffs and police, with penalties and legal sanctions. . . . their adherence to the law was the outcome of an inner desire after the beauty of Order." Lanier wishes to discount the significance of the "many names there are in art which are associated with profligacy," because "the half-way good man was but the half-way artist."[22] In this respect, Lanier's views are little removed from Shakespeare's injunction to beware as untrustworthy the man who cannot appreciate music.

These articles indicate that whereas Lanier's creative efforts in music had shifted from musical composition to a kind of scholarship, emotion was still his overriding influence. There is also evidence of his continued belief in the unity of poetry and music—that music can be used to express certain conceptions that language is too limited to convey. For Lanier, music is a larger, more universal mode of communication than language because it can express the inexpressible; therefore, society must "abandon immediately the idea that music is a species of language . . . language is a species of music."[23]

---

[20]Ibid., 301.

[21]Ibid., 275-76.

[22]Ibid., 288.

[23]Ibid., 276.

Lanier further asserts the superiority of music when he declares: "For as Shakspere [sic] is, so far, our king of conventional tones, so is Beethoven our king of unconventional tones. And as music takes up the thread which language drops, so it is where Shakspere ends that Beethoven begins."[24] There is also a repetition of the special faith Lanier has in the distinctive musical ability of Americans. He celebrates his belief that never before "was any art so completely a household art as is the music of today," and that because the American is "most completely the man of to-day, so it is directly in the line of this argument to say that one finds more 'talent for music' among the Americans, especially among American women, than among any other people."[25]

Although publication was delayed, Lanier was presumably paid for these articles, but probably not very much. They really tell nothing new about Lanier's involvement with music other than, in retrospect, it appears that he was one of the country's earliest advocates of popular musical education.[26] A more important accomplishment of the summer of 1876 was the composition of several poems, including *The Waving of the Corn*, *Clover*, and the lyrical *Evening Song*, which was set to music by Dudley Buck and, subsequently, other composers.[27] For these three pieces, Lanier earned a total of $50, half the monthly board for his family at the farm in Pennsylvania.

The Waving of the Corn is a three-stanza pastoral that mixes a mellifluous handling of the sounds of a summer field with a familiar theme: the conflict between pure nature and the "terrible towns" whose sounds denote that they are inhabited by the evil Trade. But here, as in the earlier *Corn*, the poet preaches resistance to mundane pursuits and stresses an alliance with nature. He urges the sensitive soul

---

[24]Ibid., 290.

[25]Ibid., 289.

[26]Edwin Mims points out that Lanier's interest in music education can be seen as early as 1867; in *Tiger-Lilies* he had urged that there be professorships in music just as there were in other disciplines. Mims, *Sidney Lanier* (New York: Houghton, Mifflin, 1905) 143-44.

[27]CE, 1:351, notes.

> To company with large amiable trees,
> Suck honey summer with unjealous bees,
> And take Time's strokes as softly as this morn
> Takes waving of the corn. [28]

Clover is "Inscribed to the Memory of John Keats," whose poetry Lanier loved and with whom he could easily identify; like Keats, Lanier was
passionately in love with nature, a valiant fighter against illness, and the
target of hostile critics (he agreed with the notion that the critics killed
Keats). Lanier once wrote: "To be 'John Keats at his best' with 'an American fibre' in him: that is just my desire."[29] In 1877, after Keats's letters to
his brother in Kentucky appeared in the New York World, Lanier asked
Clifford whether he had read them. "They make me think of you and me,"
he wrote. "But my lot is far brighter than Keats's."[30]

A new theme emerges in this meditative piece; it is a disciplined, flowing study in blank verse that is somewhat self-conscious in its attempt to
emulate the Romantic style ("From founts of dawn the fluent autumn day
/ Has rippled as a brook right pleasantly / Half-way to noon" [CE, 1:84]).
This is the first of several works in which Lanier uses nature as a metaphor
of the artist's struggle. Looking at the waving field, he sees in the clover
blossoms the "fair, stately heads of men / With poets' faces" (CE, 1:86).
But then a whole sheaf of artists—Dante, Keats, Chopin, Raphael, Mi-
chelangelo, Beethoven, Chaucer, Schubert, Buddha, and others—is
champed down by an ox representing the "Course-of-things." Is this the
end of these "Masters who wrought, and wept, and sweated blood, / And
burned, and loved, and ached with public shame" (CE, 1:87)? No, the
clover reassures him, it grows in God's pasture and therefore nourishes
God's plans, which appear mysterious but have ultimate meaning and order. The artist's realm, says the clover, is spiritual, and tells the poet:

---

[28]Ibid., 83-84. These are the concluding lines.

[29]Lanier, "To Mary Day Lanier," 26 January 1875, CE, 9:150. He was quot-
ing a review of Corn in the Philadelphia Evening Bulletin which made the comparison.

[30]Lanier, "To Clifford A. Lanier," 23 July 1877, CE, 9:459 n.57.

> *"The artist's market is the heart of man;*
> *The artist's price, some little good of man.*
> *Tease not thy vision with vain search for ends."*
> (CE, 1:87)

This is, of course, appropriate self-consolation for the poet, who obviously finds poor acceptance in the materialistic world, as well as being an idealistic philosophy.

This theme of the abused artist appears again in *The Bee* and *To Beethoven*, where Lanier speaks of "The praise a poet wins too late / Who starved from earth into a star" (CE, 1:89). *The Bee* takes place in the woods, where the poet lies listening to the sound of the hunt and the contrasting "fanfare" of a bee. The poet identifies with the bee, for he, too, will create something sweet if only the "worldflower" will accept him. The bee's song becomes his: "Hast ne'er a honey-drop of love for me / In thy huge nectary?" (CE, 1:92)

Indeed, what drop of honey had the world for Lanier? These poems were written during the previous bitter winter, and the battery of constant defeat could not do other than inject this note of bitterness into his work. "Prithee, abuse me not," cries the bee. "Prithee, refuse me not." But the times were no more receptive of Lanier than they ever were. Somewhat ironically, the August issue of *Scribner's* carried *A Song of the Future*, which it had purchased from him the previous fall. This is a short, lyrical piece, full of optimism, and hardly typical of the feelings he must have been experiencing at the time the poem was published:

> *Go, trembling song,*
> *And stay not long; oh, stay not long:*
> *Thou'rt only a gray and sober dove,*
> *But thine eye is faith and thy wing is love.*[31]

But efforts to "keep my pot boiling"[32] took Lanier from his rest and in search of work. At the end of September he met with President Gilman of Johns Hopkins, and they spent an evening together discussing a possible future for Lanier at the university. Gilman had been following Lanier's career and was genuinely interested in him. Lanier wrote to Peacock

---

[31]CE, 1:59.

[32]Lanier, "To Robert S. Lanier," 7 August 1876, CE, 9:390.

that "Mr. Gilman was familiar with all my poems, and . . . had thought of inviting me to a position in the University, last winter, but did not know whether I had ever pursued any special studies." Now Gilman was going to make a proposition "to the Trustees to create for me a sort of nondescript chair of 'poetry and music', giving me leave to shape my lectures into any mold I desired."[33] The trustees, however, were not as sympathetic as Gilman; they eventually decided to take no action on appointments until the following spring.

Lanier returned to West Chester, but his increasingly poor health made it all but impossible to work. Worries about his professional opportunities and finances added to the strain. He attempted to diminish these problems when writing to his father: "My career lies perfectly plain before me, and is by no means so encumbered with difficulties as many others have been. I need nothing in the world but a little money . . . and I find myself growing stronger."[34] However, it was quite the opposite, for as Mary wrote to Clifford: "Sidney has been much worse since you saw him. His cough has been more violent than any I have ever listened to."[35]

Neither poverty nor disease had loosened its hold on Lanier, and he was again in the unhappy position of desperately needing to work and yet being too ill to do so. Gilman had wanted him to remain in Baltimore for the winter, as did Asger Hamerik. On 1 November, Hamerik wrote to Lanier: "Say, are you disposed to take your old place in the Peabody orchestra this winter? You know how much your playing is appreciated by every body [sic] and all, and how glad I shall be to find the commander of the wind in his wont place."[36] Mary was more concerned than ever, fearing that if some method of relief were not procured for her husband, he would soon die. Mrs. Peacock recommended a Dr. Lippe, who was "an old, experienced German Homeopath: the foremost in the city: the pet physi-

[33]Lanier, "To Gibson Peacock," 4 October 1876, ibid., 399.

[34]Lanier, "To Robert S. Lanier," 10 October 1876, ibid., 404.

[35]Letter of 6 October 1876, ibid., 404-405 n.143.

[36]Asger Hamerik to Sidney Lanier, 1 November 1876, Charles D. Lanier Papers, John Work Garrett Library, the Johns Hopkins University, Baltimore, Maryland.

cian of Miss Cushman" and of the Peacocks as well.[37] The Laniers were urged to go to Florida, apparently by this doctor, for Mary, too, had been ill.

In November the Laniers went to Philadelphia, where they stayed with the Peacocks at their home on Walnut Street. On 12 November, the volume of poems that Lanier had prepared during the summer was published (the title-page was inscribed 1877). It contained only eleven poems—*Dedication. To Charlotte Cushman* and the ten others that had been printed in *Lippincott's* during 1875 and 1876. It is not, therefore, a very representative volume; the collection ignores Lanier's dialect poems, some lovely lyrics such as *Special Pleading* and *A Song of the Future*, and even the *Centennial Meditation of Columbia*. Nevertheless it was a successful book, if only in a modest way (half of the original edition of about a thousand copies was sold before 1881[38]).

Most of the critics reviewing *Poems* had some praise for Lanier; *Harper's* spoke of "genuine poetic genius," and the *Evening Mail* called him "the most promising of our rising poets."[39] The most popular of all the poems seemed to be *Corn*. Charles R. Anderson points out that there was "a remarkable unanimity among the reviewers," in terms of both praise and criticism. They all noted an "over-richness and obscurity resulting from a want of discipline."[40] Even Bayard Taylor, in his review for the New York *Tribune*, tempered his praise with gentle criticism. "It is still too soon to decide," he wrote, "whether Mr. Lanier's true course is to train or carefully prune" a "luxuriance" and an "apparent *abandon* to the starts and bolts . . . of Fancy." But he also said that the poems, though few, "embody as much character and thought as are usually found in the first hundred of a new poet. It is impossible to read them without feeling the presence of a clear individuality in song."[41]

While accepting Taylor's comments and those of others, Lanier was still somewhat defensive about his work; this was probably the result of

---

[37]Mary Day Lanier, "To Clifford A. Lanier," 8 November 1876, CE, 9:408.

[38]CE, 1:lii n.92.

[39]Quoted in ibid., lii.

[40]Ibid.

[41]Issue of 21 November 1876, quoted in CE, 9:412 n.158.

years of frustration, disappointment, and "a state of famine"[42] with regard to praise. Lanier was certain that he was being punished for being different. "In looking around at the publications of the younger American poets I am struck with the circumstance that none of them even *attempt* anything great. The morbid fear of doing something wrong or unpolished appears to have influenced their choice of subjects. . . . It seems to me to be a fact bearing directly upon all this, that if we inquire who are the poets that must be read with the greatest allowances, we find them to be precisely the greatest poets."[43]

However, Lanier had to divert his attention from poetry, even though it was now his primary interest: it could not support his family. Despite his poor health, he determined to rejoin the Peabody orchestra for its winter season, which commenced in December. But on 30 November, before he could leave Philadelphia, he received a mysterious envelope in the mail. It was postmarked New York and contained no message—only a $500 bill. On the envelope Lanier later wrote that "this money saved my life, by enabling me to go to Florida, where my physician had ordered me."[44] The good angels seemed to be the Peacocks, for they also kept the boys with them while the Laniers went to Florida.

Lanier informed Hamerik of his change of plans, and the director replied: "What shall we do, and how get along without you? Indeed I am afraid to direct, without . . . seeing, hearing and feeling your flute."[45] But he understood the crucial necessity of Lanier's trip and wished him well.

With their children safe at the Peacocks' and money matters at least temporarily settled, the Laniers left for Florida on 11 December. Aubrey Starke points out the irony of the journey; Lanier was now seeking in Florida "the cure he had recommended to others. The cardinal treatment of the disease which he had not followed."[46] After a ten-day trip by boat and train, they arrived in Tampa, on the Gulf coast. They settled in at the

[42]Lanier, "To Bayard Taylor," 24 November 1876, ibid., 413.

[43]Ibid.

[44]Ibid., 416-17 n.165.

[45]Asgar Hamerik to Sidney Lanier, 2 December 1876, Charles D. Lanier Papers, John Work Garrett Library.

[46]Starke, *Sidney Lanier*, 265.

Orange Grove Hotel, where they found "a large room in the second story, opening upon a generous balcony fifty feet long, into which stretch the liberal arms of a fine orange-tree holding out their fruitage to our very lips."[47] By New Year's Eve both Lanier and his wife felt stronger, and anticipated a winter free from cold and anxiety; it would also be their first winter together in five years.

---

[47]Lanier, "To Gibson Peacock," 27 December 1876, CE, 9:422.

CHAPTER X

1877:
Bread and Tears

"IF YOU HAVE EVER WATCHED a shuttle, my dear friend, being violently knocked backward and forward in a loom—never settled for a second at this end before it is rudely smacked back to the other—you will possess a very fair idea of the nature of my recent travels."[1] These words, which Lanier wrote to Gibson Peacock in the summer of 1875, describe perfectly his situation in 1877.

After spending the winter in Tampa, Lanier began a futile year of job-hunting in Washington, Philadelphia, and Baltimore. The four months in Florida had helped him regain his strength, and he had written several pleasant poems, of which seven were published over the following months. But these could not pay the bills for the idyll. The Laniers had sold their wedding silver, but medical expenses had quickly absorbed these funds. A steady job was now more necessary than ever.

Lanier was still thinking about his "French poem—The Jacquerie outburst," and he remarked in a letter to Mariquita Peacock that it would be wonderful if President Hayes "would only appoint me Consul somewhere in the South of France!"[2] Indeed, Robert Lanier had been seeking aid in securing a government position for his son; many letters were written to

---

[1]Sidney Lanier, "To Gibson Peacock," 31 July 1875, in *The Centennial Edition of the Works of Sidney Lanier*, ed. Charles R. Anderson et al., 10 vols. (Baltimore: Johns Hopkins Press, 1945) 9:224 (hereafter cited as CE).

[2]Lanier, "To Mariquita Peacock," 25 March 1877, ibid., 439.

the Secretary of the Treasury on Sidney's behalf, but nothing had any effect. Those were the days of the "spoils system," and Lanier felt himself in an awkward position. He was not involved in partisan activities and did not want to be thought of as accepting any favoritism, but he also needed work; the "service of poetry demanded the annihilation of the last vestiges of pride."[3] Bayard Taylor, who had just been named minister to Germany, went to Washington to see what he might do for his friend. Lanier himself determined to go to the capital, pinning his hopes on a treasury clerkship. He wrote to his father that "under the present furor for Civil Service reform, I would have to commence with one of the lowest places in the Department: salary $1200."[4] He would have "thankfully" accepted this job, had it been offered.

Lanier was now at a point where he absolutely craved security; although his "existence as a nomad for the last five or six years has been satisfactory enough," he was now "tired of living in a trunk."[5] He also knew that his sons needed his presence and guidance; maintaining the stability of his family was essential. Therefore, the prospect of a government position in Washington was more than agreeable. But here, as in so many other hopes, Lanier was thwarted. After months of letter-writing and knocking on doors, he finally realized that a poet could not penetrate bureaucracy. "There does not appear the least hope of success here," he wrote to Peacock from Washington at the end of September. "I am told there are rings within rings in the Department to such an extent that vacancies are filled by petty chiefs of division without even being reported at all to the proper officers. You will scarcely believe that . . . I have allowed a friend to make application to every department in Washington for even the humblest position—seventy-five dollars a month and the like—but without success." Lanier, who had previously been able to summon some optimism in the face of disappointments, was unable to do so now; his depression became almost morbid: "Altogether it seems as if there wasn't

---

[3]Aubrey Harrison Starke, *Sidney Lanier: A Biographical and Critical Study*, rpt. (New York: Russell and Russell, 1964) 280.

[4]Lanier, "To Robert S. Lanier," 3 July 1877, CE, 9:452.

[5]Lanier, "To Robert S. Lanier," 23 July 1877, ibid., 458.

any place for me in this world, and if it were not for May I should certainly quit it."[6]

Lanier's health declined markedly, as it did every time he was faced with anxiety and frustration. Yet he managed another meeting with Daniel Coit Gilman about a fellowship at the Johns Hopkins University, and even toyed with the idea of helping with Clifford's proposal to operate a small hotel in Washington. The next month he wrote that "the place of all places in the world" he desired was that of assistant librarian at the Peabody Institute, but "just at present a decline in the . . . Peabody Fund renders it impossible for the Trustees to appropriate any more money for that purpose."[7]

It is understandable that Lanier should feel despondent when the only fare life dealt him steadily was frustration. He was no unknown, no tyro; yet his talents could not win him the smallest job. He had been published in numerous journals, but none of these offered him a position. He was a man whose artistic efforts had been highly praised, who was known to thousands as the Centennial poet—but who had been consistently denied any recognition that was more than merely temporary. He was also a thirty-five-year-old family man, and the fact that he had yet to establish a permanent home troubled him more than ever. It seemed to him, as to Hamlet, that all occasions informed against him; yet he might have achieved more had he been less patient and more aggressive. His humble nature, his desire never to offend, and his refusal to compromise his ideals may have won him personal admiration, but little else. It was indeed the Gilded Age, when surface was rewarded and substance often ignored. It was a ruthless and acquisitive age that had little patience for art.

Had Lanier been a people's poet rather than a poet's poet, writing to satisfy a market, he would certainly have been more materially successful (and probably unknown today), but he steadfastly refused to sell himself—the occasional potboilers and editions of classics for children being the exceptions. Despite his sufferings, he felt that devotion to his ideals was its own reward. Each time he was pummeled by the defeats that now seemed inevitable, he responded with a quiet defiance that appears naive and pathetic, but which was undeniably courageous.

---

[6]Lanier, "To Gibson Peacock," 27 September 1877, ibid., 475.

[7]Lanier, "To Robert S. Lanier," 21 October 1877, ibid., 487.

Lanier's wanderings came to an end; once again Baltimore offered him a home. The world might not be hospitable to him as a poet, but here, as a favorite musician, he would always be welcome. He returned to the city, having been gone a year and a half, and after "the unspeakable trials and labors of the last three or four months,"[8] he finally felt "a sense of repose and of security."[9] He found an apartment on Lexington Street that was within a few blocks of the Peabody Institute, the Johns Hopkins University, an art gallery, and concert halls. The best feature of the flat was that it was also home to Mary and the three boys.

Events slowly began to turn in Lanier's favor. *To Richard Wagner* was published, and a Baltimore weekly, *Every Saturday*, commissioned a Christmas poem. The result was *The Hard Times in Elfland: A Christmas-Eve Story for Children*, in which even Santa Claus is a victim of poverty; the setting of the poem is the Laniers' own parlor. Another poem was printed in *Appleton's*, and was followed by his writing *The Song of the Chattahoochee*, one of his best works. And, though his lungs were giving him more trouble than ever, he was able to rejoin the Peabody orchestra and "play through the daily rehearsals, of two hours each, without detriment."[10] This gave him—and Hamerik—a sense of new joy and vigor.

One of the happiest events of that season was Lanier's discovery that his prison-camp comrade John Tabb was still alive. During the summer, Lanier had come upon an anonymous poem in *Harper's* called *The Cloud* and had immediately liked it. He learned that it was written by his war-time companion when he received a letter from the author in late August. Lanier excitedly replied that, having heard that Tabb had come to Baltimore for music studies, he had searched for him. "I made diligent inquiry after you, which was finally closed with the information that you had died there. I have therefore mourned you, ever since, as one never to be seen again on This Side; and you may judge, herefrom, with what pleasure I read your letter."[11]

---

[8]Ibid., 488.

[9]Lanier, "To Robert S. Lanier," 26 October 1877, ibid., 490.

[10]Lanier, "To Robert S. Lanier," 19 December 1877, ibid., 509.

[11]Lanier, "To John B. Tabb," 25 August 1877, ibid., 465.

Tabb, now teaching and studying for the priesthood, did not have the opportunity to visit Lanier until November, but the two established a lively correspondence in which they discussed, among other things of the day, each other's poetry. Finally, on 28 November, Tabb arrived at Lanier's home; it had been ten years since their separation at Point Lookout. It was an occasion for joy, but the reunion deeply troubled Tabb. He wrote to his sister that he had seen Lanier and "never have I been more cordially greeted. It did my heart good to see his face again, but it saddened me to find him so changed—I fear, poor fellow, he has not long to stay."[12]

But Lanier was now fully optimistic. After all, as he wrote to his father, if he compared his present situation to that of the previous winter when he had been virtually ordered to Florida, "when I was entirely incapable of work, and separated by a thousand miles from my children—I think you must find cause for great rejoicing and hopeful augury."[13] And there was at last justification for these hopes; Lanier was beginning his most creative period. Once again inspired by the joys of music, he would write his best poems and would fulfill his dream of teaching. With his family beside him, he could truly join the life of Baltimore as a complete citizen, for now he had his heart as well as his livelihood in the city.

---

[12]John B. Tabb to Hally Tabb, 28 November 1877, quoted in ibid., 503 n.106.

[13]Lanier, "To Robert S. Lanier," 25 December 1877, ibid., 509-10.

CHAPTER XI

1878:
A New Life

THE LANIERS BEGAN THE NEW YEAR in a new house at 33 Denmead Street in the northernmost part of Baltimore.[1] It was a symbol of the stability that Lanier had found, and his situation presented a great contrast to his condition of two winters past. His new exuberance was poured into letters to his confidants Taylor and Peacock. To Taylor he wrote: "I think I could wander about the house—we have nine rooms!—for a month with my hands in my pockets, in supreme content with treading upon my own carpets and gazing at my own furniture. When I am on the street there is a certain burgher-like heaviness in my tread . . . I am a man of substance, I am liable, look you, for water-rates, gas-bills, and other important disbursements."[2] The same day he told Peacock: "No man is a Bohemian who has to pay water-rates and a street-tax. Every day when I sit down in my dining-room—*my* dining-room! I find the wish growing stronger that each poor soul in Baltimore, whether saint or sinner, could come and dine with me."[3]

---

[1]Denmead Street is now 20th Street; the door of Number 33 is in Gilman Hall on the Homewood campus of the Johns Hopkins University, Baltimore, Maryland.

[2]Sidney Lanier, "To Bayard Taylor," 6 January 1878, in *The Centennial Edition of the Works of Sidney Lanier*, ed. Charles R. Anderson et al., 10 vols. (Baltimore: Johns Hopkins Press, 1945) 10:3-4 (hereafter cited as CE).

[3]Lanier, "To Gibson Peacock," 6 January 1878, ibid., 5.

Lanier quickly reestablished contact with his old Baltimore friends who also became warm friends to Mary and the boys. Charley, the eldest, was enrolled in the Pen Lucy School run by Richard Malcolm Johnston, a writer and a native Georgian. Lanier had known Johnston, who was twenty years his senior, when he had been in Baltimore previously, but now their friendship deepened. Johnston's country home was a short ride from Denmead Street, and visits were easily arranged. Because they had so many things in common, including a love of music, the families became very close.[4] In February, Lanier began teaching part-time at Pen Lucy.

Rejoining his comrades at the Wednesday Club for its lively meetings, Lanier probably participated in the customary highlight of the weekly sessions, a rendition of Verdi's *Anvil Chorus*. Ottilie Sutro, daughter of the club's founder, Otto Sutro, writes that everyone participated in this performance, "with coal scuttles, andirons, tea-kettles, tin pans, any and every old thing wherewith to make noisy substitution for anvils."[5] There is a sketch commemorating this event, penned in 1863, before Lanier's time; Henry Wysham is pictured, playing the flute while other men are singing, playing violins or horns, and solemnly clanging buckets and wine bottles. A drawing which includes Lanier is an elaborate sketch by Dr. Adalbert J. Volck (a dentist who was also a very versatile artist) made in 1878. It depicts an imaginary parade of the members, "Returning victorious, after having lightened the pathway through this vale of tears, with *Art*, *Music*, the *Drama* and *Convivial Groceries*." The musicians comprise the first group in the march, with Otto Sutro in the lead, followed by a group of ten, including Wysham and Lanier, who has his flute tucked under his left arm. Volck's inscription under this part of the parade notes that "Official authority, upheld by esprit de corps, keeps step to the Music of the Future."[6] Lanier's health probably kept him from too much socializing, but perhaps

---

[4]Francis Taylor Long, "The Life of Richard Malcolm Johnston in Maryland," *Maryland Historical Magazine* (December 1939): 313.

[5]Ottilie Sutro, "The Wednesday Club: A Brief Sketch from Authentic Sources," *Maryland Historical Magazine* (March 1943): 61.

[6]The sketch is reproduced in vol. 10 of CE (frontispiece). The sketch of the Wednesday Club's "Anvil Chorus" is in the Sutro Collection of the Maryland Historical Society.

he did play for some of the many soirees given each season in the club's rooms on North Charles Street.

There had been changes in the musical life of the city while Lanier had been absent. The first American Beethoven Memorial Festival had been presented at the Peabody Conservatory in 1877 as a benefit for erecting a statue of the composer in Bonn. Also in 1877, Baltimoreans had heard their first telephone broadcast of a concert held in New York, the "Grand Telephonic Concert at the Masonic Temple."[7] Asger Hamerik's ambitious concert programming, combined with decreasing funds, had resulted in growing deficits for the Peabody; although it was not an economic success, the orchestra seemed more popular than ever, still attracting large audiences. The Peabody Institute was growing physically, too; in 1878, the old building was repaired and a new art and music wing was completed.[8]

Lanier's new life was quite improved. He worked on "some unimportant prose matter for pot-boilers," an occasional poem, and nursed his plans for completing his *Jacquerie*.[9] He could ride down to the Peabody on the Charles Street tramcar in just a few minutes and work for a while at his usual seat in the institute's library before rehearsals. Or he could walk across Mount Vernon Square to the home of Sarah and Edgeworth Bird, who had long been helpful to him. Mrs. Bird, another Georgian, had lived in Baltimore since 1869; she was wealthy, and her handsome brownstone home was the center of culture and elegance.[10] Desiring to assist Lanier in his quest for work, she devised a plan that March: Lanier could give a series of lectures in her home and she would provide the audience. Lectures of this kind, "sometimes called 'parlor classes,' were quite popular in that decade, and evidence the fact of the city's cultural rebirth and stimulus."[11]

---

[7]Ortmann, "Musical Baltimore in the Seventies," (Baltimore) *Evening Sun*, 16 July 1935.

[8]Ray Edward Robinson, *The Peabody Conservatory: An American Solution to a European Musical Philosophy*, 2 vols. (Baltimore: Peabody Conservatory, 1968) 1:230, 2:3.

[9]Lanier, "To Gibson Peacock," 30 January 1878, CE, 9:16.

[10]CE, 1:379-80, notes.

[11]John Saulsbury Short, "Sidney Lanier, 'Familiar Citizen of the Town,'" *Maryland Historical Magazine* (June 1940): 132. The Birds' home still stands.

This was, as Lanier wrote to his father, "a very flattering invitation" that "came without any previous knowledge of such intention on my part." He would deliver a series of lectures on eight consecutive Saturday afternoons to about thirty "cultivated ladies." His chosen subject was "The Sonnet-writers from Surrey to Shakespeare," and he approached the task with total delight. "There seems every probability," he wrote, "that this will be the beginning of a pleasant and profitable business for me."[12] He was finally correct in his predictions. The lectures were successful, and especially for Lanier. Mrs. Bird, with clever wisdom, invited Dr. Gilman to attend one of the sessions. "He gladly came," she recalled, "and he, too, was charmed. At the close, he said to me, 'I never heard a more charming lecture,' and with a smile, 'I certainly hear a great many.' "[13]

The Peabody Institute was also impressed and invited Lanier to participate in its fall "Shakspere course." Of forty lectures, Lanier was to deliver twenty-four; six other lecturers were to present the remaining sixteen. The status provided by the affiliation with the Peabody Institute was probably the deciding factor in Lanier's ultimate acceptance as a teacher by the Johns Hopkins University; and since Gilman had much to do with securing the lectureship at the Peabody, this experience became an important test for Lanier.

Endeavoring to expand his intellectual horizons as well, Lanier had borrowed and read three books belonging to Bayard Taylor: James Russell Lowell's *Among My Books*, Swinburne's *Atalanta in Calydon*, and *Leaves of Grass* by Walt Whitman. A note sent by Lanier to Taylor on 3 February— Lanier's thirty-sixth birthday—indicates that this was his first reading of Whitman. He wrote that he could find nothing new in the Swinburne and Lowell volumes, "But LEAVES OF GRASS was a real refreshment to me— like rude salt spray in your face—in spite of its enormous fundamental error that a thing is good because it is natural, and in spite of the world-wide difference between my own conceptions of art and its author's."[14] As he had first heard Wagner's music a decade after it had been introduced to America, so he was a trifle late in discovering Whitman. It is peculiar that

---

[12]Lanier, "To Robert S. Lanier," 10 March 1878, CE, 10:26.

[13]Quoted in ibid., n.31.

[14]Lanier, "To Bayard Taylor," 3 February 1878, ibid., 18.

it took him so long to read the work of the only other living American poet who had musical sensibilities; more so, since several critics who disliked the *Centennial Meditation of Columbia* compared it to *Leaves of Grass*.[15]

Initially, Lanier found pleasure in Whitman's poetry, although his Puritan side could not reconcile itself to Whitman's earthiness. In May 1878, Lanier wrote to the older poet, asking for a copy of the book. "How it happened that I had never read this book before—is a story not worth the telling," he apologized. But he also offered "grateful thanks for such large and substantial thoughts. Although I entirely disagree with you in all points connected with artistic form . . . my dissent in these particulars becomes a very insignificant consideration in the presence of that unbounded delight which I take in the bigness and bravery of all your ways and thoughts. It is not known to me where I can find another modern song at once so large and so naive. . . . I beg you to count me among your most earnest lovers, and to believe that it would make me very happy to be of the least humble service to you."[16] Whitman replied only with a short note, but by 1878 he was past the height of his career and was in poor health. Nonetheless, in his third Hopkins lecture, Lanier derided Whitman; the Puritan had proved dominant and was supported by the sentiment of academic circles, where Whitman was generally unaccepted.

In 1881 Lanier would say: "I complain of Whitman's democracy that it has no provision for sick, or small, or young, or plain-featured, or humpbacked, or any deformed people, and that his democracy is really the worst kind of aristocracy, being an aristocracy of nature's favorites in the matter of muscle." He called Whitman a "dandy-upside-down" who affectedly "throws away coat and vest, dons a slouch hat, opens his shirt so as to expose his breast, and industriously circulates his portrait, thus taken, in his own books." He protested against "the Whitman school . . . against a poetry which has painted a great scrawling picture of the human body and has written under it, 'This is the soul'."[17] But in 1878, that year of growth and rediscovery, Whitman was to Lanier a pleasant revelation.

---

[15]CE, 4:ix n.6.

[16]Lanier, "To Walt Whitman," 5 May 1878, CE, 10:40.

[17]*The English Novel*, CE, 4:53-54.

Upon rejoining the Peabody orchestra, Lanier was immediately involved in solo work, and apparently his virtuosity had not been dimin-
ished by a year of musical inactivity. On 2 March, at the seventh concert
of the season, Lanier appeared as soloist in a concerto by the contemporary Danish composer Emil Hartmann (1836-1896). Originally scored for
violin and orchestra, it had been arranged for flute and orchestra; it would
seem likely that Lanier had arranged the music himself, but this is never
mentioned. Relating the events of the concert to Clifford, he was proud
of his achievement, but his earlier passionate outbursts were now sup-
planted by a more professional reserve. "The composition was a very difficult one, and many believed it could not be rendered on the flute at all.
The result however was satisfactory: the close of the first movement brought
down the house . . . the orchestra broke forth in applause and the leader
stepped down from his place and congratulated me. Of course this gave
me much pleasure, and I played the two remaining movements, with even
greater success. . . . at the end a wonderful basket of flowers was handed
up to me mid hearty applause."[18] The Baltimore *Gazette* reported that Lanier's performance "showed not only a mastery of the instrument, but a
refined and cultivated musical intelligence. His concerto was received with
great applause."[19]

Perhaps the most visible evidence of the orchestra's devotion to Lanier is a concert presented on his behalf on 6 April 1878 at Lehmann's
Hall in Baltimore. The concert, "given by the Peabody orchestra, Ma-
dame Nanette Falk-Auerbach, and Miss Elisa Baraldi, to Sidney Lanier,"
was played before a full house. The program included the Mendelssohn
Piano Concerto in G minor (with Mme. Falk-Auerbach as soloist), a nocturne from Hamerik's opera *La Vendetta* (Opus 20), and the Prelude to Act
IV of his *Tovelille* (Opus 12), the *Swedish Wedding March* of August Sod-
erman, and Beethoven's *Symphony #8*.[20] But the highlight of the evening
was Lanier's own solo in another performance of the Hartmann concerto.
Lanier "was very heartily applauded, his beautiful flute performances al-

---

[18]Lanier, "To Clifford A. Lanier," 3 March 1878, CE, 10:23.

[19]Article of 4 March 1878, quoted in ibid., 23-24 n.28.

[20]Original concert program, Charles D. Lanier Papers, John Work Garrett Library, the Johns Hopkins University, Baltimore, Maryland.

ways affording great pleasure. Altogether the concert testified in a satisfactory manner the appreciation of Mr. Lanier as an artist and
gentleman."[21]

"Such was his popularity with the members of the orchestra," writes
Isabel L. Dobbin, who was a student at the Peabody Conservatory while
Lanier was there, "that when asked by someone (I believe I was the person) to assist in a benefit concert for Mr. Lanier, they consented in enthusiastic unison, and a more complete *accord* than usual. While he, dear
hospitable soul, insisted on offering them a supper out of the proceeds,
though he was greatly in need of the money."[22] Such a gesture would have
been typical of Lanier, but apparently the musicians insisted that he keep
the money, for two weeks later he reported to Clifford that the concert
had provided him with $164.[23]

More musical honors awaited Lanier in May, when he was selected to
be on the music committee for the Maryland Musical Festival. The festival concerts, under the baton of Asger Hamerik, were held at the Academy of Music on 27-29 May and were reported each day by Lanier for the
Baltimore *Sun*—unfortunately without a byline. The festival was apparently a huge success, attracting large audiences and many dignitaries, including the governor of Maryland. The large orchestra, composed of
musicians "exclusively of Baltimore" (including Lanier), was joined by a
chorus of three hundred singers from the city's numerous musical organizations. The festival also featured many programmatic works, including
Niels Gade's *Symphony #1* ("On Sjølund's Fair Plains")—a robust and
lyrical work based upon folk idioms—Hamerik's *Jewish Trilogy*, and the
Siegfried Idyll of Wagner; one concert was devoted entirely to the works,
orchestral and choral, of Beethoven.[24]

Lanier's report of the musical proceedings—from a description of the
flowers on stage to the ticket receipts—also includes programmes for some
of the pieces and, inevitably, Lanierian philosophizing. The same age, he

[21]Baltimore *Sun*, 8 April 1878, 4, col. 2.

[22]Isabel L. Dobbin, "Lanier at the Peabody," *Peabody Bulletin* (April-May 1911): 5.

[23]Lanier, "To Clifford A. Lanier," 21 April 1878, CE, 10:33.

[24]CE, 2:324-26.

says, which has produced Darwin, Spencer, and Huxley, "has produced also Beethoven in music and the landscape school in painting. For these three phenomena—the modern scientist, musician, and landscape painter—are merely three developments, in different directions, of one mighty impulse which underruns them all."[25]

Although the musical experiences of the spring were exciting, Lanier's true joy lay in his academic prospects. He was establishing a new reputation for himself, for in the Baltimore city directory he was listed as "writer." The lectures at Mrs. Bird's were a success from the start, with attendance steadily growing. April 6 was Lanier's special day; it began with a lecture on "The Melody of Sound" and culminated with his complimentary concert. This was the lecture Gilman attended, and at its conclusion he approached Lanier "in the most cordial way, with congratulations and an invitation to deliver it at the University."[26] By the middle of May, the Lecture Committee of the Peabody Institute had appointed Lanier to teach a "Shakspere" course twice weekly from November 1878 to the following April. Lanier would have the entire summer in which to prepare the lectures.

It was a summer well spent. Lanier worked steadily at home and at the institute's library, which was rich in volumes of the Elizabethan poetry he loved and wished to emphasize in his lectures. He also worked on his own poetry and, in July, sent "three poems, hot from the mint"[27] to publishers. One of these was The Marshes of Glynn, the work for which Lanier is most famous. He had written it for an anthology in the "No Name" series published by Roberts Brothers in Boston; the origin of the series was commercial strategy: by making readers guess the authors' identities, the books would become a topic of conversation and more people would want to purchase them.[28] The editor of the anthology, G. P. Lathrop, had written to Lanier: "The names of the authors will not appear; but it is intended to make this collection representative of the best poets in this country. . . .

[25]"The Maryland Musical Festival," ibid., 321.

[26]Lanier, "To Clifford A. Lanier," 21 April 1878, CE, 10:33.

[27]Lanier, "To Robert S. Lanier," 13 July 1878, ibid., 53.

[28]Aubrey Harrison Starke, "An Omnibus of Poets," Colophon (NY) 4, pt. 16 (March 1934): n.p.

After a short interval, the contributors will be at liberty to announce the authorship of their pieces. . . . I should prefer a short piece with some piquant conceit for a basis; something also with Southern coloring."[29] Lanier reported proudly to his father that after he had read the poem to his friend Richard Malcolm Johnston, the latter declared it "the greatest poem written in a hundred years."[30]

Lanier also wrote several papers on "The Physics of Poetry," for which *Scribner's* paid $300 in September; edited an edition of *Froissart's Chronicles* "with the uninteresting and objectionable parts expurgated, and accompanied by a historical and explanatory introduction, designed specially for boys"[31] (it was a collaboration between the adventurous and Puritan sides of Lanier); plus he worked on a book on prosody. His overwork concerned Mary, who wrote to Clifford's wife Wilhelmina that she expected Sidney to "die at his desk. He has written enough within five months to kill a stronger man."[32] Although the strain on Lanier's health worried her, she was happy that he had the work and enjoyed it. The joy that he had known as a student at Oglethorpe University two decades earlier, when he had dreamed of Europe and the scholar's life, was now being reborn. "Such days and nights of glory as I have had!" he wrote exuberantly. "I have been studying Early English, Middle English, and Elizabethan poetry, from Beowulf to Ben Jonson: and the world seems twice as large."[33]

An entirely new phase of Lanier's life began at a few minutes before noon on Saturday, 2 November 1878, as he climbed the broad steps of the Peabody lecture hall on West Monument Street, two blocks from Mount Vernon Square.[34] As with many of his other ventures, this lecture series would prove a financial failure, but it was a success in terms of furthering his reputation. The twenty-four lectures that Lanier delivered were to cover Shakespeare in

---

[29]G. P. Lathrop to Sidney Lanier, 20 April 1878, quoted in CE, 10:53 n.66.

[30]Lanier, "To Robert S. Lanier," 13 July 1878, ibid., 53.

[31]Lanier, "To Robert S. Lanier," 24 August 1878, ibid., 64.

[32]Mary Day Lanier to Wilhelmina Lanier, 10 September 1878, quoted in ibid., 64 n.80.

[33]Lanier, "To Bayard Taylor," 20 October 1878, ibid., 72.

[34]The building still stands, housing offices of the Diocese of Maryland.

> a very symmetrical presentation . . . in his relation to
> The Anglo-Saxon Time,
> Middle English Time
> His own Time, *and*
> The Present Time.[35]

But Lanier's desire to present his audience "with a vivid picture, first of the influence of Shakspere's time upon him, and then of his influence upon us,"[36] was ambitiously expanded to include almost the entire history of the English language and related subjects. Several early lectures were devoted entirely to a study of the technique of verse, so that Lanier could base the groundwork of understanding upon his own definitions. He began with his basic definition that "every formal poem is primarily a series of sounds,"[37] and continued with a discussion of the elements of verse. These lectures became the nucleus of *The Science of English Verse*, which he wrote the next summer.

His listeners were given a feast of *Beowulf*, Chaucer, "The Wife in Middle English Poetry," the English Renaissance sonneteers, four lectures on "The Domestic Life of Shakspere's Time," plus an examination of the plays and an introduction to Lanier's own theory of verse. All this was not without order; Lanier was not trying to glut his audience with an encyclopedic syllabus. In his introduction to the lectures in *The Centennial Edition of the Works of Sidney Lanier*, Kemp Malone notes that Lanier limited his topics within the scope of his historical area and then presented comparisons of works in order to illustrate a point. As an example, Malone cites Lecture 7, "*Beowulf* and *Midsummer Night's Dream*." Here Lanier studies changes "in the English attitude toward nature."[38] From *Beowulf*, he moves to Chaucer's *The Flower and the Leaf* (which he feels is "worth all the *Canterbury Tales* put together"), to Gavin Douglas's early sixteenth-century *The Palice of Honour*, to the *Mirrour for Magistrates*, and

---

[35]Lecture 6, CE, 3:9.

[36]Lecture 5, ibid., 7-8.

[37]CE, 3:300.

[38]Kemp Malone, ibid., xx.

on to *A Midsummer Night's Dream*, ending with his own *Nature-communion* in Baltimore's Druid Hill Park. As Malone states, "Shakespeare is not central; he is a point on a temporal line of *development*, a line which passes through him and continues indefinitely."[39]

If these lectures are approached as literary studies by a musician, the most interesting sections are those on "Pronunciation of Shakspere's Time" and "The Music of Shakspere's Time." Within these studies there is a foreshadowing of Lanier's lectures at Johns Hopkins and his treatise on music and poetry.

The first of the two lectures on "Pronunciation of Shakspere's Time" begins with an outline of ideas with which Lanier had been working for years. In his essay "From Bacon to Beethoven," written two years earlier, he had asserted that language is "a species of music." He takes this idea further in this study, and would elaborate upon it again in *The Science of English Verse*; each time he addressed himself to this question, he had the benefit of additional study to fortify his statements.

In this, the sixteenth lecture of the series, he declares that "the only proper view of verse is that which regards it as a phenomenon of sound." He introduces his idea that "the alphabet [is] on exactly the same plane with the common European musical system of notation. . . . the letters of the alphabet constitute a system of notation for the tone-color of sounds." Because Lanier sees the basic elements of sound, musical and spoken, as being duration and pitch, each syllable of a word may be taken as "a sort of large sign of tone-color." The implication of this in a study of Shakespeare is that, unless the modern reader understands which tone-color was indicated by certain syllables in Elizabethan English, he is "color-blind," as is "a musician who in studying the music of a given period should be ignorant of the pitch or time-value indicated by a given note. . . . unless we know these points of difference we are in effect color-blind" to many of Shakespeare's effects.[40] Lanier cites many good examples of places where an understanding of Shakespeare's pronunciation obviously elucidates his intentions; the humor of Falstaff's statement in *Henry IV*, "If reason were as plenty as blackberries, I would give no man a reason upon compulsion,"

---

[39]Ibid., xx-xxi.

[40]Ibid., 168-69.

is apparent when it is understood that "reason" was pronounced so as to suggest a pun on "raisin."

Lanier also digresses a great deal from his opening statements, which could have been presented much more succinctly. But he had a thesis to present, one which had been preoccupying him for years, and the lecture was not an inappropriate time to introduce it. He would continue to work on the idea of the musical notation of verse to the point that when he began writing *The Science of English Verse*, a book-length exposition, he would be able to do it in six weeks.

There must have been a special delight in researching and presenting the two lectures on "The Music of Shakspere's Time," for here was an age thoroughly permeated with music, from "the organ, the stately motet and involute canon, the Puritan's psalm, the jolly catch, the melodious madrigal, the tinkling of citterns, gitterns, lutes, and virginals, the soft breaths of recorders, the louder strains of clarion, sackbut, shawm, hautboy, trumpet, cymbal and drum" to the "simply enormous" number of ballads sung in the streets.[41] And Lanier, whom Robert E. Spiller calls a "belated Elizabethan,"[42] would naturally have been in accord with the concept of music held by Shakespeare and his contemporaries—the idea of the "music of the spheres," the mystic and moral implications of music.

Lanier is quick to point out Lorenzo's famous injunction in *The Merchant of Venice* against the man who "hath no music in himself," and matches it with a proverb he found quoted in books of Shakespeare's time: "Who loves not music, God loves not him." He applauds the importance music had in that time, the significance attached to it, and its general enjoyment, shared by everyone from the songwriting Henry VIII to the common people singing as they worked. What an appealing picture of musical England Lanier portrayed, and how he must have wished that nineteenth-century America could have been of a like temperament.

In his descriptions of Elizabethan musical instruments and compositions, Lanier reveals the broadened scope of his own musical understanding. "One great and cardinal distinction of modern music as opposed to the music of Shakspere's time is that the composers of that period did *not*

---

[41]Ibid., 205.

[42]*The Oblique Light: Studies in Literary History and Biography* (New York: Macmillan, 1948) 212.

address themselves to the invention of new tunes so much as to the *contrapuntal treatment of old tunes.*"[43] He then explains and illustrates the technique of counterpoint, knowledge he has gained through his studies and orchestral experiences—knowledge which is so markedly absent in his early compositions.

What impressed Lanier so much was that Shakespeare not only "loved music with sincere passion" and often "wrote passages which indicate gleams of insight into its mysteries," but that the abundance of music and musical imagery in the plays is evidence of the central importance of music for the entire age. Certainly he thought it noteworthy that the monarch herself found music to be such an essential element of court life that she had fifty-four musicians on "the royal pay-roll."

In one of the interesting asides which he was fond of delivering, Lanier observes that while the English have always loved music, there has "never yet developed a single great English composer of music," certainly none of the stature of a Bach or Beethoven. He directs the same question to women and concludes that "*never yet* is not *never at all . . .* perhaps women and Englishmen will both write immortal music in the ages to come."[44] This is a logical extension of the progressive idea he introduced in his 1876 essay, "The Orchestra of To-Day," that women should study orchestral instruments as well as the genteel piano—doubtless these suggestions found favor with the large number of women attending the lectures.[45]

Lanier had apparently been as charming a lecturer as possible, given the formidable scope of his syllabus. No doubt, he suggested to the class at the concluding meeting, many of the lectures had been trials and antagonisms, but he hoped that since life, like music, creates harmony from opposition, "perhaps your fineness of nature might turn these antagonisms, too, into music."[46] His self-effacing concluding remarks, consciously or otherwise, fitted nicely into the Elizabethan tradition of

---

[43]CE, 3:214.

[44]Ibid., 209.

[45]Kemp Malone believes the class was entirely composed of women, with men occasionally attending (ibid., xi n.16).

[46]Ibid., 307.

apologizing to the audience; and Lanier was like a modern Puck, asking his listeners to "Give me your hands."

The course was, from all evidence, educationally but not financially successful. The provost's report notes that "the entire proceeds" were given to Lanier (who was in charge of all its business, and not just his own lectures), "to be used as he might see fit to secure the completion of the course, the Institute furnishing room, heat, light, and attendance, but incurring no other responsibility."[47] Yet what Lanier did not earn in salary, he earned in reputation. The Peabody lectures established him as a painstaking and conscientious scholar. In his class preparations, he had meticulously investigated the volumes in the Peabody Institute's new library (opened on 30 September 1878) in his efforts to be thorough.

He combed the shelves, discovering such works as Mathis Lussy's *Traite de L'expression Musicale*, A. J. Koch's *Neue Tonlehre, Colour-Music* by D. D. Jameson, and a current work recently translated into English, *Die Lehre von den Tonempfindungen* by Hermann L. F. von Helmholtz.[48] Inspired by Helmholtz's discoveries in acoustics, Lanier sought other books on the subject, even persuading the librarians to let him examine new volumes that were still in their shipping cases. One of the librarians, John Parker, recalled Lanier's interest in works published by the Early English Text Society, the Chaucer Society, the Percy Society, Shakespearean criticism, and certain new reprints of Elizabethan literature.[49]

Lanier also had, in his personal library, recent editions of Chaucer (1872) and Shakespeare (1876); recent studies of Shakespeare; John Tyndall's *Sound—A Course of VIII Lectures*, revised by the Royal Institution of Great Britain (1867); *The Laws of Verse*, a treatise linking mathematics and poetry, written in 1870 by Hopkins's eccentric mathematics professor, James J. Sylvester; and Pietro Blaserna's *The Theory of Sound in its Relation to Music* (1876).[50] There are sufficient references to these books in

---

[47]Peabody Institute, *Twelfth Annual Report of the Provost to the Trustees* (1 June 1879) 14-15.

[48]Frederick Kelly, "Sidney Lanier of the Peabody Institute," *Peabody Bulletin* (1939): 37.

[49]CE, 7:lvii. The Peabody Institute library was one of only a few American subscribers to receive these reprints of Elizabethan literature.

[50]CE, 1:lxx n.138; 7:liii.

Lanier's works to indicate that he did read them. However, as a man of diffused interests and only newly returned to the discipline of scholarship, Lanier could not be expected to produce error-free work. "The marvel is," writes Aubrey Starke, "that working in haste and excitement his scholarship is as accurate as it is, that his notes, references, and citations are generally reliable."[51]

Full of enthusiasm about the Peabody lectures, Lanier conceived of yet another project, even before he met his first class: the transformation of contemporary lecture courses into "Schools for Grown People." He had proposed the idea of an "Institute" for adult education to Dr. Gilman; Lanier would be director and Gilman the chairman of the advisory committee. By the end of September 1878, he had abandoned the idea. Yet he had been so inspired by the success of the lectures at Mrs. Bird's and by the "evident delight with which grown people found themselves receiving systematic instruction in a definite study," that he related to Gibson Peacock his hope of expanding the reach of the Shakespeare course to Philadelphia and Washington. His premise was solid—"Men and women leave college nowadays just at the time when they are really prepared to study with effect"—but the project never materialized.[52] The only thing that did emerge was a printed circular, which listed categories of study: "The Household," "Natural Science," "Art," and "School of English Literature" (similar to the Shakespeare course at the Peabody). Under "Art," only one lecturer was listed—Lanier—addressing himself to a pet subject: "Four Lectures on the Modern Orchestra, with special reference to women as orchestral players."[53] Despite the fact that this particular plan did not come to fruition, it caught the interest of Gilman; and, as Kemp Malone points out, "the extension work which from the beginning was a prominent feature of the Hopkins program developed largely along lines marked out by Lanier, who thus became one of the fathers of academic adult education in America."[54]

---

[51] Aubrey Harrison Starke, *Sidney Lanier: A Biographical and Critical Study* (reprint, New York: Russell and Russell, 1964) 325.

[52] Lanier, "To Gibson Peacock," 5 November 1878, CE, 10:76-78.

[53] Ibid., 77 n.92.

[54] CE, 3:viii.

Whatever frustration encroached in the early fall was recompensed by the success of the Peabody course and a major poetic triumph, which occurred at the end of the year. This was the publication of *The Marshes of Glynn* in the anthology, *A Masque of Poets*. The volume contained poems of Christina Rossetti, Richard Watson Gilder, Bayard Taylor, James Russell Lowell, Emily Dickinson, and Louisa May Alcott. Several major poets of the day—Longfellow, Holmes, Whittier, and Whitman—were ignored in favor of dozens of very minor, now-forgotten authors.

In general, critics found little to praise in the *Masque*, but if any work was admired, it was *The Marshes of Glynn*.[55] Actually, Lanier himself was not impressed with the volume, calling it "an intolerable collection of mediocrity and mere cleverness," stating that he "could find only four poems in the book."[56] Yet if the volume was not an aesthetic success, it certainly was a commercial triumph. The temporary anonymity imposed by the publishers was also a boon to Lanier, for the new year found him at home gleefully recording the critics' guesses about the authorship of his work. The poem, Lanier wrote to his father, "has imposed upon some of the Boston Critics in the most delightful manner. Some of their guesses about it are amusing enough. . . . Several had guessed me as the author of the Marsh poem: others attributed it to Jean Ingelow, one to Tennyson."[57]

An editorial in the *Atlantic Monthly* (probably written by Howells), which had successfully kept Lanier's work from its exclusive pages, commented upon the mystery poem: "There is a fine Swinburnian study called The Marshes of Glynn, in which the poet has almost bettered in some passages, his master's instructions."[58] On 3 January 1879, Longfellow, having learned Lanier's identity, wrote to him requesting permission to include the poem—with credit to Lanier—in a volume called *Poems of Places*.[59] Lanier was delighted, not only with the prospect of having his work reprinted and reaching a larger audience, but with his acceptance by Boston critical circles.

---

[55]Starke, "An Omnibus of Poets," n.p.

[56]Lanier, "To Gibson Peacock," 21 December 1878, CE, 10:88.

[57]Lanier, "To Robert S. Lanier," 1 February 1879, ibid., 97.

[58]Quoted in Starke, *Sidney Lanier*, 316.

[59]CE, 10:96-97 n.7.

But the letter that Lanier had been most expectantly awaiting—for more than two years—arrived in February, in time to be a present for his thirty-seventh birthday. It was a formal invitation to join the Johns Hopkins faculty. Gilman had finally been successful in convincing the university trustees of the desirability of adding Lanier to the faculty roster. They had "unanimously voted" to invite him to lecture on English literature during the academic year of 1879-1880, and would pay him a salary of $1,000.[60] Lanier was even taken aback, for as he told his father, he "knew nothing of any such intention" on the part of the university. His short letter of acceptance to Gilman is warm and calm, but privately he was elated. All the activities of the spring and the summer were now illumined by the prospect of joining, as a peer, a group of renowned scholars.

The ensuing frenzy of activity unfortunately did much to undermine Lanier's health. Rehearsals, concerts, library work, the lectures, and writing left very little time for the precious rest he needed. In March, his poetic tribute to Bayard Taylor, who had died in Berlin in December 1878, appeared in *Scribner's*, and his essay on Bartholomew Griffin—"A Forgotten English Poet"—was published in the *International Review*, a New York-based journal.[61] It is significant that *To Bayard Taylor* is the only poem Lanier had published in 1879 (contrasted with eight in 1878), and he apparently wrote only one new poem, *Owl Against Robin*, in 1879; his time and attention were almost totally devoted to his new academic career. He also edited *The Boys' King Arthur* from Malory; although he loved the tales of chivalry he found in Malory and in Tennyson, he still resented having to do this work while he had so many original ideas to develop. His frustration is evident in a letter to his father: "If I had not learned to murmur at nothing, I should be inclined to complain at the cruel fate which keeps me editing other men's works to boil the pot, when my head is so full of books of my own that I sometimes have a sense that I must actually fly into fragments if I do not lessen the inward accumulation."[62] He further exhausted himself by traveling to New York and Boston to confer with pub-

[60]Lanier, "To Robert S. Lanier," 5 February 1879, ibid., 98.

[61]CE, 6:387.

[62]Lanier, "To Robert S. Lanier," 6 May 1879, CE, 10:111.

lishers about the possibilities of producing a series of textbooks (based upon his lecture material), but the quest was unsuccessful.

By the time the Peabody semester was over and the Baltimore concert season had ended, Lanier and his wife were both in poor health, which made the idea of spending the summer away from the city very desirable. Mary had spent a month of the previous summer at a farm in Rockingham Springs, Virginia, and the Laniers decided to go there with the boys. "It is a wretchedly rough and primitive place," Lanier wrote to his brother, "but the mountains are there, and many trees, and I long for these so pitifully."[63] The resort, which was popular with many Baltimoreans, was about twelve miles from Harrisonburg, in the Shenandoah Valley, shadowed by the Blue Ridge mountains and freshened by mineral springs. The Laniers found invigorating air and pleasant company here. Lanier amused himself with horseback riding, playing his flute for the other guests, and delivering an address to the knights at a local "tournament." He also worked six hours every day, and at the end of their six weeks' stay, he had almost completed the manuscript of *The Science of English Verse*.

---

[63]Lanier, "To Clifford A. Lanier," 8 June 1879, ibid., 123.

CHAPTER XII

Lanier
at Johns Hopkins

WHEN LANIER RETURNED TO Baltimore in mid-September he was far from rested, yet he immediately launched into the frenetic pace which he had set for himself—there were so many things he wanted to do and he knew he had a limited time in which to do them. He planned a series of college-level textbooks—a "Student's Chaucer," "The First English Comedies," and others—but only *The Science of English Verse* was written.

A month before beginning his duties at Hopkins, Lanier obtained additional "school-engagements." One of these was what Lanier called "a unique course in philosophico-historico-esthetico-literary studies," presented to "a class of ladies who have passed college days and are pursuing post-graduate studies for the pure aim of an increase of their culture."[1] This seems to have been similar to the class at Mrs. Bird's, given at a school run by "The Misses Adams" on West Madison Street, not far from Mount Vernon Place. Other schools at which Lanier taught during the year were Mrs. Singleton's Eutaw Place School, Mrs. Jones's Mount Vernon Institute for Girls, and, again, the Pen Lucy School.

When Lanier arrived for his lectureship, he already knew most of the Hopkins faculty—not a difficult matter, since there were only six professors and a few associates.[2] He knew Professor Basil Gildersleeve, the em-

---

[1]Sidney Lanier, "To Clifford A. Lanier," 9 October 1879, in *The Centennial Edition of the Works of Sidney Lanier*, ed. Charles R. Anderson et al., 10 vols. (Baltimore: Johns Hopkins Press, 1945) 10:147 (hereafter cited as CE).

[2]Daniel Coit Gilman, "The Launching of a University," *Scribner's* 31 (March 1902): 332.

inent classicist, from the Wednesday Club, as well as Dr. Gilman. The principles on which the university was based and the faculty Gilman had selected assured Lanier of an atmosphere conducive to and receptive to original thought. Gilman believed "the object of a university was 'not so much to impart knowledge to the pupils, as to whet the appetite, exhibit methods, develop powers, strengthen judgment, and invigorate the intellectual and moral forces' "[3]—a philosophy consistent with Lanier's love of learning as an exciting and vital quest.

When Lanier was at Hopkins, there was no campus—just a few brick residences on North Howard and Ross streets in the heart of the city. Johns Hopkins's bequest for the founding of the university was that it ultimately be built on the grounds of his country estate; until this could be accomplished, the school expanded within its city neighborhood. The school was only a few blocks west of the Peabody Institute, but to Lanier it was a great distance, which, as he entered the red brick, mansard-roofed Hopkins Hall, he had covered triumphantly.

On 28 October, Lanier met his first class—150 students who came to learn about "English Verse, especially Shakspere's." His first set of lectures was open to the public, and his reputation was such that twice as many tickets were requested for the opening lectures than could be distributed.[4] Lanier was apparently a captivating lecturer, for the hall was always full, and the average attendance at his classes was much higher than at others. Gilman recalled that Lanier always "did his best—and his best was very good—to inspire and instruct those who came within the sound of his voice."[5]

His first lecture included some exalting thoughts on literature. "I believe that it is the business of Literature to keep the line of men touching shoulders as we move up through the darkness; I believe that the Poet is specially in charge, here below, to convert Learning into Wisdom; I believe that the advance of Science necessarily implies the advance of Po-

---

[3]Quoted in "Johns Hopkins University," an entry in the *American Cyclopaedia Supplement* (1880), attributable to Lanier; CE, 3:412.

[4]Lanier, "To Robert S. Lanier," 29 October 1879, CE, 10:151.

[5]"Pleasant Incidents of an Academic Life," *Scribner's* 31 (May 1902): 617.

etry . . . as thus the poet was the Preacher of the Past so he must be the Preacher of the Future."[6]

He began his treatment of Shakespeare in much the same manner as the Peabody lectures, with a discussion of the elements of verse and how an understanding of verse affected the modern reader's understanding of Shakespeare. It was in 1874, he told the class, that the *New Shakspere Society* proposed to determine the chronology of the plays by the "Metrical Tests." In these tests, Lanier saw "the dim beginning of a criticism which will no longer flounder brutally in the dark, but which will work with at least the possibility of becoming a science . . . resting upon the sure basis of observed facts."[7] This new era of Shakespearean criticism coincided with the development of a scientific theory of verse, he told the group, and proceeded to explain his own "Science of English Verse"; the bulk of the material presented in the first nine lectures is contained in Lanier's own book of theory.

This is the theory towards which he had been working for years, a theory whose origins lay in his discussions with Professor Woodrow as they rode through the Georgia countryside when Lanier learned about the beauties of scientific application. It was this theory—the one with which he had lived all summer—he now presented: that all poetry is sound and, as sound, may be studied and notated metrically as music.

At the same time that Lanier was presenting these ideas to his class, he was preparing *The Science of English Verse* for its publication by the firm of Charles Scribner. However, when a question arose concerning the intended audience of the book, Lanier and Scribner had differences of opinion. Initially, Lanier wanted his work to be "mainly for *the general reader* but capable of being used as a text-book," but now—December 1879—he conceived of the book as "*purely* a text-book, not appealing to the general reader at all."[8] This would, of course, make the volume much more of a risk, since the audience would be substantially reduced. By the end of the month, trusting in Scribner's practical expertise and being very eager to see the work in print, Lanier inquired as to "how much change in the pres-

---

[6]CE, 3:318-19.

[7]Ibid., 316-17.

[8]Lanier, "To Charles Scribner," 6 December 1879, CE, 10:157.

ent form would make it accord" with the "idea of a popular treatise."⁹ In January, the book went to press.

The winter wore on, with Lanier working at a "killing pace." In addition to his two lectures each week at Hopkins, he gave seven others at the various small schools. He also began to prepare two more "boy's" books, two volumes of poems, and a study of Chaucer and Shakespeare. However, his body could not keep pace with this punishing schedule, and the new year found him very ill; Mary, still in a weakened condition and plagued with eye trouble, tended him. But as soon as Lanier was able to be up and about, he went to New York to confer with Scribner.

Any possibility of rest was eliminated by the opening of the Peabody orchestra season and, with this renewed involvement with music, Lanier began to write about music. The first concert, presented Saturday, 31 January, featured Anton Rubinstein's *Ocean Symphony*, Emil Hartmann's *Raid of the Vikings*, and the *Hungarian Rhapsody #2* by Franz Liszt. The Hartmann work, noted the Baltimore *Sun*, "was written only last year, and will be played to-night for the first time in America." The *Sun* went on to say that, at the direction of Asger Hamerik, "Mr. Sidney Lanier has written an interpretation, in order to render more intelligent the pleasure of those" who will attend the concert.¹⁰ The newspaper then included Lanier's program notes to the Rubinstein and Hartmann works, as a preview of the evening's concert. The presentation was apparently a success, for on Monday the *Sun* reported a "large and attentive" audience.

The spring concerts featured many works of programme music, indicating a sustained interest in this form of composition. The concert of 4 February included Berlioz's *Roman Carnival Overture* and excerpts from *Faust*; a week later the *Slavonic Rhapsody #1* by Dvorak was performed. A March highlight was Hamerik's own *Fourth Norse Suite*, "composed in Baltimore 1876-1877." In April, the orchestra played the *Norwegian Rhapsody* of Johan Svendsen, another contemporary Scandinavian, and gave a repeat performance of the *Ocean Symphony*.¹¹

⁹Lanier, "To Charles Scribner," 29 December 1879, ibid., 168.

¹⁰Baltimore *Sun*, 31 January 1880, 1.

¹¹Original programs. Charles D. Lanier Papers, John Work Garrett Library, the Johns Hopkins University, Baltimore, Maryland.

Perhaps inspired by this exciting music and encouraged by the publication of his essay, "The Orchestra of To-Day," in the April issue of *Scribner's* (although the magazine had bought the article in November 1876), Lanier proposed to write a "Handbook for Orchestras." Part of this book, he told Charles Scribner, would be in response to the many requests for information on carrying out the essay's suggestion that women play orchestral instruments. Although he admired Lanier's outline of the book, Scribner felt that his firm would find few customers for such a work. Undaunted, Lanier decided to submit his plan to "some music-publisher, who would have direct connections with its audience and would know its chance for a market. I suspect, myself, it is a doubtful book: but the subject matter has such a fine parallelism with that of *The Science of English Verse*, and would enable me to develop so many principles hinted at therein, that I should like to write the work, if I can possibly make it pay only expenses."[12] Whether Lanier actually proposed this "Handbook" to any other publisher is unknown, and only fragments of what might have been his plan for the book have been found.

Academics had also received its share of Lanier's time that spring. On 8 February, he began teaching a course, this one limited to Hopkins students, on Chaucer and Shakespeare. "The aim of the lecturer," read the course description, "will be to awaken an interest in the poems under review solely as works of art";[13] the course was apparently designed to introduce non-English majors to early English literature.

Two honors related to the university came to Lanier in February. He wrote an ode which he delivered on the fourth Commemorative Day, 23 February 1880; his praise of the young institution, and of its devotion to science and literature, is couched in language often self-consciously occasional:

> And here, O finer Pallas, long remain, —
> Sit on these Maryland hills, and fix thy reign,
> And frame a fairer Athens than of yore
> In these blest bounds of Baltimore —

The image of Baltimore surpassing ancient Athens as a center of culture

---

[12]Lanier, "To Charles Scribner," 16 May 1880, CE, 10:195.

[13]CE, 10:172n.9.

is something of an overstatement, but it reveals the genuine love Lanier felt for his adopted city. The poem also states Lanier's own academic philosophy—that to understand great writers, one must study not criticism, but the works themselves.[14] The second acknowledgment was his commission to write an article on the university for the *American Cyclopaedia Supplement*, published in New York by the firm of Appleton-Century. The entry bears no signature, but it is undoubtedly by Lanier.[15]

The Hopkins course ended on 15 March, the Peabody season on 23 April. It had been a semester of growth and excitement, but the constant, unrelaxed activity had severely taxed Lanier; his features had sharpened, his hair and beard gone grey. But on 12 May a new arena of activity opened: *The Science of English Verse* was published.

The book fell into the established Lanierian pattern by arousing immediate controversy, one which has quieted but not abated. In general, the more thoughtful reviewers gave the book favorable reception. But one paper claimed that "a drearier book was never written," and another thought the volume "ought to be instructive, for it is very dull"[16]—both with some justification, for while *The Science of English Verse* is more than just interesting, it is less than intensely sensational. However, it is unfair to expect a scientific treatise to read like a novel. The negative criticisms piled up. The New York *Evening Post* missed the whole point of the book, filling its review with what an exasperated Lanier called "the climax of silly misrepresentation."[17] The Chicago *Times* called Lanier's theory "exceedingly far-fetched"; the *New York Times*, opining that "we are somewhat in danger of being 'scienced' to death," accused Lanier of "pedantry and precision," and went beyond this even to ridicule Professor Sylvester's *Law of Verse*.[18] However, as Paull Franklin Baum, editor of Lanier's writings on music, points out, *The Science of English Verse* was not, as Lanier knew, for the general reader and could not have been dealt with equitably or competently by general book reviewers.

---

[14]"Ode to the Johns Hopkins University," CE, 1:133-35.

[15]CE, 10:176 n.16.

[16]Quoted in CE, 2:xxxi n.29.

[17]Lanier, "To Gibson Peacock," 1 June 1880, CE, 10:203.

[18]Quoted in CE, 2:xxxi n.29.

There were also many positive and comprehending reviews. The Boston *Courier* hailed the book as "a fresh source of pride in American literary scholarship," and Francis F. Browne, editor of the *Dial* in Chicago, wrote a long article in which he concluded that Lanier's book was "beyond question the most striking and thorough exposition yet published on the technics of English poetry."[19] The "Editor's Literary Record" in *Harper's* called the book a "scholarly and elaborate treatise," and, after providing a succinct outline of Lanier's theory, recommended it to "the attention of the amateur, the student, and the professional poet, by reason of the thorough technical knowledge it imparts, and its keen analysis of the phenomena and constituents of verse."[20] Thomas Wentworth Higginson, in a general article on Lanier for the *Chautauquan* magazine, later reported that by 1887 *The Science of English Verse* had become such a popular book at the Harvard library that it had to be placed "upon the list of books to be kept only a fort-night."[21] Twentieth-century literary critics are similarly divided in their opinions of the merits and defects of Lanier's work,[22] but little attention has been accorded the volume in the last thirty years.

Of what ultimate importance is Lanier's theory of verse, and how does it enhance an understanding of his verse? The general verdict of scholars over the years is that Lanier's poetry is far better than his theory, that the often lush quality of the former is preferable to the exaggerations and inaccuracies of the latter.

Lanier develops in his book the various premises that he had previously asserted about poetry as sound, with the result that in analyzing the duration of this sound, he is actually discussing English quantitative verse, though he never calls it by this name. Lanier realizes that he is at the end of a long line of poetical theorists, though he feels that, before the advent of his book, "it still cannot be said that we possess a theory, or even a working-hypothesis, of the technic of English verse."[23] With regard to En-

---

[19]Quoted in ibid., xxxii n.30.

[20]*Harper's* 61 (October 1880): 796-97.

[21]*Chautauquan* 7 (April 1887): 417.

[22]A survey of criticism of *The Science of English Verse* is provided in Paull Franklin Baum's introduction to CE, 2:xxx-xxxvii.

[23]CE, 2:6.

glish quantitative verse, he is aware of the "learned absurdities" of the "Areopagus" group (Sir Philip Sidney, Edmund Spenser, Fulke Greville, Gabriel Harvey) in proposing "a scheme for reducing the English language into subjection to the classic laws of quantity." He knows the passage in Sidney's *An Apology for Poetry* that declares quantitative verse "more fit for music, both words and tune observing quantity, and more fit lively to express divers passions by the low and lofty sound of the well-weighed syllable."[24] However, Lanier makes no mention of Thomas Campion's *Observations in the Art of English Poesy*, which also defends quantitative verse; Lanier mentions Campion in his writings only once—as the author of the words of a masque given in 1614.[25] Campion, as poet, composer, and theorist, is the one historical figure most parallel to Lanier, and it is odd that Lanier did not study Campion's own experiments in verse.

Coleridge, in his preface to *Christabel*, speaks of the poem as seemingly, but not actually, irregular because of its "being founded on a new principle" of counting accents, not syllables. But Lanier replies that this principle has been "employed, as far as it can be, in English poetry for more than a thousand years; and the very nursery-rhymes and folk-songs of our tongue present us everywhere with applications of it."[26] So Lanier knew he was not the first to discuss at length the rhythmical basis of English.

However, he was the first to make such an extensive comparison of the rhythms of speech and the rhythms of music, illustrating his comparisons by applying musical notation to verse.[27] Paull Franklin Baum believes that Lanier "was the first student of the phenomena of English verse

----

[24]Lanier cites the sentence before this one in his text, CE, 2:6. See Sidney's essay in *The Prose Works of Sir Philip Sidney*, ed. Albert Feuillerat (reprint, Cambridge: Cambridge University Press, 1962) 3:44.

[25]"Lanier Genealogy," CE, 6:363. In this account of the history of the Laniers, Sidney Lanier mentions a Nicholas Lanier (1568-c. 1646-1649) who was a court musician in the time of James I of England. He composed a particular masque for the wedding of the Earl of Somerset in 1614, and "words to this masque," writes Sidney Lanier, "were written by Dr. Thomas Campion."

[26]CE, 2:11.

[27]Campion had also drawn parallels between measurements of words and musical notes.

. . . to start with an analysis of the acoustic values of words,"[28] applying
his knowledge of recent work in sound and his expertise in music. Lanier
repeats his statement that verse is "a set of specially related sounds" when
read aloud, and a set of related "signs of sounds" when read from the printed
page. Therefore, reading poetry in a book differs from hearing it spoken
in that the reading eye "merely purveys for the ear."[29] He then draws an
analogy between the elements that constitute the sounds of music and of
verse, and they are the same: rhythm (dependent upon duration), time
(dependent upon pitch), and tone-color, or timbre (dependent upon such
constituents as rhyme, distribution of vowels and consonants, and alliteration). The major difference, to Lanier, between music and verse is that
in music the elements listed are conveyed by "a series of *musical sounds*"
and in verse by "a series of *spoken words*."[30]

Some of his points are coherently made and little argument can be
found with them. In discussing "the times of ordinary talk, or speech-mel-
odies," he explains how inflection can give meaning to the words, or
change the impression, of an entire phrase. He gives a good illustration of
this in one of his miscellaneous writings: "Let any one think how many
times he has misconstrued letters he has received, letters written by the
sender to be read in a certain tone of voice, but received by the reader in
some alien mood which caused him to imagine a different tone."[31] In *The
Science of English Verse*, he speaks of Charlotte Cushman's readings as
"really nothing more than performances of speech-tunes," one person's
voice successfully conveying an array of characters and actions—when an
entire play is seen by the ear. His assertions that the effect of a poem can
be altered through the manipulation of rhyme and rhythm are acceptable.

But another point, which Lanier makes at the beginning of the first
chapter, is difficult to believe. Formal poetry, he says, "impresses itself upon
the ear as verse only by means of certain relations existing among its component words considered purely as sounds, without reference to their associated ideas. . . . All ideas may be abolished out of a poem without

---

[28]CE, 2:xl.

[29]Ibid., 21.

[30]Ibid., 41.

[31]"On Music," ibid., 340.

disturbing its effect upon the ear as verse." For example, if words in a foreign language—even if they have nothing to do with the original meaning
of the poem—are substituted for the English, the verse will be "unim-
paired" as long as the foreign words "preserve the accentuation, alliteration, and rhyme."[32] Lanier made himself a rather blatant target with these
sentiments, especially placing them as he did in the first paragraph of the
first chapter. What he actually meant was that the sense of a poem should
lie within its sound; for instance, he asked Professor Gildersleeve to "read
Greek poetry aloud to him for the sake of the rhythm and the musical effect,"[33] although he did not understand Greek. Conversely, he would have
expected the sense of his poetry to be comprehensible to a non-English-
speaking listener.

In attempting to adapt musical notation to words, Lanier employs as
his basic premise the idea that "All English words are primarily rhythmical" (51). He goes on to explain the six "orders" of rhythm, each of which
is a "sound-group": the syllable (which can correspond to a note), the foot
(or bar or measure), the phrase, the line, the stanza, and the "final
rhythmical group embracing all these"—the poem (76). This is followed
by 150 pages of examples, from early poetry through Shakespeare to modern writers, of poetic scansion fitted to musical notation. Some are ques-
tionable, his analysis actually "forcing the analogy of music and verse."[34]
One instance of this is the following application to Hamlet's soliloquy:

which should actually read more like this:

---

[32]Ibid., 21. Subsequent page references will be given within the text.

[33]Basil Gildersleeve to Edwin Mims, quoted in Edwin Mims, *Sidney Lanier*
(New York: Houghton, Mifflin, 1905) 239.

[34]CE, introduction, 2:xlii.

Lanier's reading of Anglo-Saxon verse such as *Beowulf* and *The Battle of Maldon* (acknowledged as an inspiration by the Anglo-Saxon scholar J. C. Pope), however, is competent and logical. One interesting point of reference is that Lanier twice gives a musico-rhythmical analysis of Tennyson's *Break, Break, Break* (80, 108) in 3/8 meter, yet his own musical setting of it is in 4/4. But perhaps if he had set the poem to music at a later date, after developing not only more musical sensitivity but also a scientifically oriented theory, it would have fallen into triple-meter.

The ideas contained in *The Science of English Verse* are intriguing but also repetitious and often belabored; terseness was never one of Lanier's virtues. However, he was working within the context of scientific inquiry, and he knew that nothing less than a completely thorough investigation and explanation of his subject matter would suffice; he also wanted the general reader as well as the advanced student to grasp his meaning, hence the repetition. Above all, Lanier saw his work as an application of scientific principles to an existing understanding of poetry; he did not intend this book as a "how to" manual for rhyming amateurs. He knew that many might take the work to be a set of rules for composition, and that he would be criticized for it, so his final chapter reaffirms the superiority of the aesthetic sense. "For the artist in verse," he states, "there is no law: the perception and love of beauty constitute the whole outfit. . . . In all cases, the appeal of poetry is to the ear; but the ear should, for that purpose, be educated up to the highest possible plane of culture" (244).

How does Lanier's own poetry respond in terms of this ear-culture? Aubrey Starke notes the results of two studies made in the 1920s that seem to find little connection between Lanier's theory and practice. Ruth Willcockson's "Rhythmical Principles and Practices of Sidney Lanier"[35] concludes that the only tenet to which Lanier apparently adhered was his last, that of the poet's ultimate freedom from rules.[36] Another University of Chicago student, Pearl Elizabeth Brown, finds that his verse demonstrates "not so much the creation of new elements as the effective and varied marshalling of old forces,"[37] concluding that Lanier was perhaps radical in

---

[35]M.A. thesis, University of Chicago, 1928.

[36]Aubrey Harrison Starke, *Sidney Lanier: A Biographical and Critical Study* (reprint, New York: Russell and Russell, 1964) 354.

[37]Quoted in ibid., 355.

theory but conservative in his own art. An overview of his poems will show that those based upon the song-concept can easily be notated musically, but not the later meditative and experimental verse.

The Science of English Verse is the result of Lanier's lifelong desire to unite music and poetry, and here he could do it under the sanctioned umbrella of science. In American Prosody, Gay Wilson Allen states what can be considered a representative judgment by critics who have thoughtfully examined Lanier's theory: he finds the "artificiality" of the musical notation system "objectionable" and the major hypothesis of the theory "untenable," but concedes that "a great part of his treatise is scientifically correct, and all of it is challenging and suggestive."[38] The book is generally recognized as a pioneering work, but is also generally ignored in studies of prosodic theory, American or otherwise. It is, of course, far less interesting than Lanier's poetry; therefore, in order to determine the extent of Lanier's success in creating a union of the arts, a more fulfilling examination may be made of the actual musicality of his mature poetry.

---

[38](New York: American Book Co., 1935) 283.

CHAPTER XIII

The Musicality
of Lanier's Later Poetry

LANIER FOUND IN MUSIC and musicians a natural focus for the tribute of words; yet it was also just as natural for music to become so involved in his writing process that he was eventually composing poetry not just about melody and tone, but with it. In the dozen years between *Life and Song* (1868) and *Sunrise* (1880), Lanier's poetry absorbed music steadily and increasingly, transforming it from a subject to a creative process until the verse was no longer a vehicle for describing music, but music itself.

Most of these poems were written while he was in Baltimore. Accordingly, Lanier never wrote about music from afar, except *Life and Song*, but always under its direct influence and inspiration. Perhaps with the strains of a recently played symphony still reverberating in his consciousness, Lanier began to compose so that his nature-poetry became musical creations. In some cases, the extreme emotionality that music always created within Lanier spilled over onto the pages of his verse, creating what critics have termed an excess, "lush" quality. That the role of music was sometimes a self-conscious one cannot be denied; yet it is equally true that without music, Lanier's verse would also have been without its charm and would likely be completely forgotten today.

How successfully did Lanier integrate musical elements into his work? Of his musically oriented poems, those about musicians are much less successful than those in which music is the medium rather than the subject. His poem dedicated to the Swedish diva Christine Nilsson (1871), one untitled work evidently dedicated to Baltimore singer Jenny Busk (1874),[1] one to Peabody colleague Nanette Falk-Auerbach (1878), one to Richard Wagner (1877), and two to Ludwig van Beethoven (1876)—all reveal evident love for his subjects. But they are written formally, in conventional verse styles, rather strict and stiff, self-conscious in construction. The one exception in Lanier's poetry about music is *The Symphony*, which does convey musical meaning through the manipulation of sound, albeit in an occasionally rudimentary fashion.

Lanier's genius as a creator of synaesthetic verse, first evident in *Corn*, appears in full flower in his mature nature-poetry: *Song of the Chattahoochee*, *The Marshes of Glynn*, and *Sunrise*. The parallels between music and verse are most closely drawn in these poems, and Lanier's words form something more than poetry—an evocative realm of rich sound.

It must also be remembered that Lanier's poetry is for the ears, not the eyes. In writing verses for the ear, Lanier is again a composer, this time for voice alone; but he is also returning to the original conception of poetry as a spoken art. Because Lanier's works are designed to be heard, their effect is more sensuous than intellectual. Only a very few people can experience music by reading an orchestral score; the music must be played and listened to before sense can be made of the notes and pleasure obtained. In the same way, Lanier's poetry must be read aloud for ideal effect.

Song of the Chattahoochee was written in Baltimore in November 1877, and Lanier was so pleased with it that he had "some suspicion that it is the best poem I ever wrote."[2] It describes the journey of the Chattahoochee River from Habersham County in northern Georgia, to Marietta and Atlanta, flowing west to form the western boundary of the state, then down through Florida to the Gulf of Mexico. Yet the river is more than a topographical feature—and this is true of all of Lanier's nature-poetry—it is a metaphor of life. As the river narrates its journey past various obstacles, it reveals that the call of "the voices of Duty"[3] is more powerful than any

---

[1]*The Centennial Edition of the Works of Sidney Lanier*, ed. Charles R. Anderson et al., 10 vols. (Baltimore: Johns Hopkins Press, 1945) 1:378, notes (hereafter cited as CE).

[2]Sidney Lanier, "To Robert S. Lanier," 30 November 1877, CE, 9:501.

[3]CE, 1:103-104.

mundane hindrance or distraction. But this is not the source of the poem's beauty. Its magic lies in the true singing quality of the verses. The tonal suggestiveness of the words, the steady but far from monotonous rhythm, and the refrain echoing with "the hills of Habersham" and "the valleys of Hall," all contribute to a complete aural experience.

The emphasis upon repetition, alliteration, and onomatopoeia underscores the musical effects of this poem. Speaking of its passage past narrow banks and thick foliage, the river relates how

> *The rushes cried* Abide, abide,
> *The willful waterweeds held me thrall,*
> *The laving laurel turned my tide,*
> *The ferns and the fondling grass said* Stay
> (13-16)

This liquid, caressing sound gives way to stately and measured sound as the river passes the tall forests, and becomes correspondingly harsh as rocks agitate the path of the water:

> *The white quartz shone, and the smooth brook-stone*
> *Did bar me of passage with friendly brawl*
> (33-34)

The musical qualities of *Song of the Chattahoochee* are far from subtle, to the point that it is always in danger of being read or recited in a sing-song fashion, something which would be extremely difficult to do with *The Marshes of Glynn. Song of the Chattahoochee* has often been compared with Tennyson's *The Brook* (a poem with which Lanier was familiar), and Philip Graham has compared the musical effects of Lanier's poem with those of Coleridge's *Song of Glycine*, finding them alike in "tone-color."[4] Graham assumes that, as an admirer of Coleridge, Lanier knew this song; however, there is no concrete evidence to suggest that Coleridge's poem served as inspiration for Lanier or that Lanier definitely knew the piece. But certainly Lanier's familiarity with the river, and his sensitivity to the music of nature, provided sufficient background for the composition of the poem.

Curiously, the work with which *Song of the Chattahoochee* is most similar is a musical work written about the same time: Bedrich Smetana's *The*

---

[4]"A Note on Lanier's Music," in *Studies in English* (Austin) 17 (1937): 107-10.

Moldau (Vltava). This is one of the most popular nineteenth-century "tone poems," describing the progress of the river Moldau from a trickling mountain stream, through woods, past meadows, and over rapids, until it flows broadly past the city of Prague. Lanier did not know the work, yet it is remarkable how closely the journey of his own river parallels the one of Smetana; the poem could almost serve as a programme for the music. Reading *Song of the Chattahoochee* while listening to *The Moldau* will reinforce an appreciation of Lanier's ability to create a sound-picture in verse.

A more tangible musical parallel exists between Lanier's most famous poem, *The Marshes of Glynn*, and one of his favorite musical works, the *Symphonie Fantastique* of Hector Berlioz. Many similarities between the two works can be noted, strongly suggesting that Lanier's familiarity with Berlioz's work helped shape the poem. Both works are "visionary," but of course in quite different ways; Berlioz's is a hellish portrayal of opium-induced dreams, while Lanier's meditation reveals that man can find internal peace in nature. But in structure, if not in conception, there is a definite relationship between the two works.

The *Symphonie Fantastique*, according to Berlioz's own programme, depicts the dreams of a young artist obsessed with a "Beloved" who haunts and torments him. Though each movement is distinctly different, describing subjects as disparate as a ball, a pastoral scene, a march to the scaffold, and a witches' sabbath, they are connected by one melodic theme that recurs in various forms in each section. Lanier was aware of this because a programme to the music was printed in the Peabody concert program; he also wrote to his wife that in the *Symphonie Fantastique*, "as difficult and trying a piece of Orchestration as was ever written," each movement "centereth about a lovely melody, repeated in all manner of times and guises, wh. representeth the Beloved of the opium-eating musician."[5] This recurring melody is what Berlioz termed the "idée fixe," a constant motif. So the symphony is doubly programmatic; each movement, describing in tone a stage in the artist's obsession and its related experience, is an individual tone poem. But the recurrent "idée fixe," as it weaves through the movements, unites them to form a compelling whole.

Lanier's revelation, unlike that of Berlioz's artist *persona*, is affirmative, strengthening, and full of joy. As he tries to fathom the significance

---

[5]Lanier, "To Mary Day Lanier," 21 December 1873, CE, 8:437.

of the marshes, he also moves through several stages, guided in each by his own "idée fixe": this is the repetition (with some variation) of "the length and the breadth and the sweep of the marshes of Glynn." The incantorial sound of the line itself suggests the impressive expanse of the marsh.

As Berlioz uses different instrumental tonal colors to create setting (for example, the English horn to open the pastoral "Scène aux champs"), Lanier uses color and tone to develop his atmosphere.[6] There is constant interplay of light and dark—the time is twilight—sunlight and shadow. The poem opens with "glooms," "intricate shades," dim and dark woods, and "braided dusks"; all of these half-tones are resolved by the end of the poem when night, which neutralizes all shades, falls. But before this happens, the marshes offer Lanier an understanding of his universe; he exults in the colors revealed by the sun: green marsh-grass, the blue main, and a "rose-and-silver evening glow" (l. 88). Where he was troubled before by "the weighing of fate and the sad discussion of sin" (l. 63), he is "suddenly free." The marshes, now signifying an embodiment of God's infinite plan, show him the paradox of experience: there is ultimate good in everything. The marshes are made "to suffer the sea and the rains and the sun" (l. 67), but they are yet beautiful and steadfast, symbolizing the "good out of infinite pain" (l. 69) and "sight out of blindness" (l. 70) that come with faith. Lanier sees the marsh not as a desolate and barren area, but as the one place where land, sea, and sky meet and mesh in a harmony of nature.

The effect of the poem as a whole is similar to that of the third (the pastoral "Scène") and first movements of the *Symphonie Fantastique*. The first movement ("Rêveries, Passions") begins calmly and builds in excitement as the "idée fixe" of the Beloved gains intensity. So too *The Marshes of Glynn* opens quietly as the poet moves through the silent and dim woods on his way to the edge of the marsh, but becomes more exuberant as the poet's confidence and faith increase. He once feared the overwhelming sweep of the marshes, which suggested the magnitude of the dreariness of earthly existence, but now his "belief overmasters doubt," and he declares: "I know that I know" (l. 28).

The meters of the poem are varied, but they blend easily, and lines of varied lengths flow gently into each other. There is a primary metrical

---

[6]*The Marshes of Glynn*, CE, 1:119-22.

pattern, though: rhymed couplets of pentameter and hexameter lines. Lanier seems equally comfortable with short, strong, and emphatic lines:

> Oh, now, unafraid, I am fain to face
>> The vast sweet visage of space.
> To the edge of the wood I am drawn, I am drawn,
> Where the grey beach glimmering runs, as a belt of the dawn,
>> For a mete and a mark
>> To the forest-dark: —
>>> So:
>>> (ll. 35-41)

as with longer, mellifluous, and sensuous lines:

> Inward and outward to northward and southward the beach-
>> lines linger and curl
> As a silver-wrought garment that clings to and follows the
>> firm sweet limbs of a girl
>>> (ll. 51-52)

The only regularly metered part of the poem is a hymn-like section towards the end. These eight lines (ll. 71-78) contain the key image of the marsh hen. As the hen builds a nest in marsh grass that sends its roots deep into the "watery sod," so Lanier will build a nest of faith "on the greatness of God" (l. 77). He has found the roots of his faith in God's world of nature, and it is this faith which has, for him, transformed the marshes from a frightening expanse to "the greatness of God."

The "idée fixe" returns again at the end of the poem; the poet now feels he understands the marshes, but has no knowledge of the "forms that swim and the shapes that creep / Under the waters of sleep" (ll. 102-103). He only wishes he "could know what swimmeth below when the tide comes in / On the length and the breadth of the marvellous marshes of Glynn" (ll. 104-105). As Berlioz's "idée fixe" continues to haunt him, even to the end of the symphony, so Lanier's returns to confront him with the ultimate meaning of life. There is some understanding which actually is marvelous and which, it is suggested, we cannot have.

Lanier's last completed poem, *Sunrise*, is also a tone poem and complements *The Marshes of Glynn*, for it moves from darkness to light, from troubled night to inspiring day. The musical feeling in this poem is even more powerful. Like the "Rêveries" of the *Symphonie Fantastique*, this has a visionary and dreamlike quality.[7] It depicts the poet waking to a dawn that promises communion between his soul and the sun, a premonition and acceptance of death. This is presented not through simple narrative, but through the mingled voices of the soul and several elements of nature.

The poem can be divided into six segments of varied length. The introduction (ll. 1-18) and conclusion (ll. 182-93) are the shortest. Four longer sections lie between; each of the first three is a "voice" of nature, and these combine in a fourth section (ll. 149-81), a hymn to the sun. The voices—those of the woods, the marsh, and the sea—can be heard as distinct musical voices or lines, eventually uniting in one strong harmony. These voices can be interpreted, musically, in several ways.

They may be understood as individual instruments playing solos before combining as an ensemble. Here Lanier may have been utilizing his knowledge of the polyphonic construction of music, knowledge he gained in the orchestra. When a piece of music is heard in its entirety and never fragmented, a multiplicity of sounds is heard as one. The music is comprehended as a total aural sensation; individual voices not involved in solo passages are rarely heard (perhaps, in the case of a violin or piano concerto, an individual instrumental voice does make an impression). But sitting within the orchestra, the listener begins to understand the complex patterning of composition; the conductor pauses in rehearsal and concentrates upon the strings, or the winds, or the brass, and the other players listen while looking at their parts and hear how other voices are designed to mesh with their own. A good musician always listens to other players and accepts the notes he has to play as his individual contribution to one ensemble sound. This is also how a musician gains an added dimension to his own musical appreciation; when it is his turn to sit in the audience, he can hear both the total sonorous impact of the piece and the smaller voice of his instrument weaving through the harmonies. A flutist will always be sensitive to flute notes when he listens to a band or orchestra, and a bass player will always feel the lowest timbres beneath any music he hears.

In *Sunrise*, Lanier works backwards. He has experienced the joy of a new day before, but now he has become aware of the various sensuous components of the hour. He hears first the whispers of the leaves; then

---

[7]This is influenced to some extent by the 104° fever from which Lanier was suffering. CE, 1:366, notes.

the silent breathing of the marsh; and finally the flowing of the ebb tide. Only after he has become aware of each element of nature involved in the scene can he absorb the scene as a whole.[8]

Sunrise could be compared to a skillfully constructed string or wind quartet, in which the dominant voice or melody may shift, for instance, from violin to viola to cello, while the other instruments maintain integral lines of their own; they never merely accompany, but combine to form a rich tapestry of sound. Their independent lines are also dependent upon the entire ensemble for a fulfilling sound. Therefore, when Lanier hears the whispering and sifting of the leaves, the marsh and the sea are neither absent nor silent; and when he shifts his attention to the rippling water, the woods do not cease their murmur—the poet has simply become attuned to a different voice.

In the introduction, the poet is called from sleep by the voices of nature. This is a mini-overture in which the succeeding themes are suggested in brief introduction:

> *The little green leaves would not let me alone in my sleep;*
> *Up-breathed from the marshes, a message of range and of sweep,*
> *Interwoven with wafture of wild sea-liberties, drifting*
> (ll. 3-5)

Thus the voices of leaves, marshes, and sea are presented in the order of their entrances.

After waking, the poet first addresses the leaves (ll. 19-57) and listens to their whispering, singing, and murmuring (ll. 39-46), hoping to understand the meaning of silence and the importance of patience. As he moves to the beach, he hears another voice, within the woods, of an owl (l. 54). The "reverend Marsh" is next approached as it is "distilling silence" (l. 60), a silence which is "ministrant" (l. 71). The marsh has another type of silent music; its many interwinding streams repeatedly reflect the heavens, and therefore the marsh is also "A rhapsody of morning-stars" (l. 83).

------

[8]The individual entrances of four voices, followed by an ensemble effort, suggest the idea of a fugue, but without *overlapping* entrances this idea is undermined (for example, if the beginning of the marsh's description referred to the previous "woods" section).

A bridge passage (ll. 86-97) prepares for the quietly building sound of the sea and for the vision of sunlight. The beauty and silence of the pre-dawn hour creates a "bow-and-string tension" (l. 88) that anticipates the awakening of the day: "Oh, what if a sound should be made!" (l. 86).

Motion, sound, and light now come from the sea (ll. 98-140). The key image within this section reintroduces Lanier's bee-symbol—the bringer of sweetness, life, and light. The aureate dome of the day rises over the marsh and sea, followed by the golden sun-bee rising to its zenith. Since the sun is rising directly over the water, it is the sea that is "Forever re-vealing, revealing, revealing" (l. 146) its majesty.

Now Lanier connects all the various thematic lines; "with several voice, with ascription one, / The woods and the marsh and the sea and my soul" (ll. 149-50) sing together in praise of the sun. The "voice" of the soul has not been specially mentioned, nor does it have to be, for it has been sounding all along, an *obligato* to the other sounds. If the soul were absent, the whispers and sighs of nature would not be heard at all. This hymn to the "innermost Guest / At the marriage of elements" (ll. 155-56), the "chemist of storms" (l. 168), and "manifold One" suggests that this illu-minating force is God, and the following coda, or conclusion, of the poem is an affirmation of faith.

In the conclusion (ll. 175-92), emphasis shifts to the poet—that is, to the soul. For some, the advent of the day means "The worker must pass to his work in the terrible town" (l. 177), but the poet fears not "the thing to be done":

> I am strong with the strength of my lord the Sun:
> How dark, how dark soever the race that must needs be run,
> I am lit with the Sun.
> (ll. 179-81)

But Lanier does not leave the reader on this note; he concludes with nightfall and, therefore, with a return to sleep and the opening situation of the poem. This time, sleep will be easy since he has come to a harmo-nious understanding with his universe during the day. Lanier's musical groping for the ethereal in nature, as in *Wind-Song*, is tangibly rewarded through its combination of verbal meaning and musical sound.

During his later years, Lanier did not cease writing short, lyrical poems (if anything, these were made even more lyrical by his musical knowl-edge). *A Ballad of Trees and the Master*, also written in 1880 and intended to be placed within *Sunrise*, is one example. It is a religious poem whose internal rhymes and unobtrusive repetition, as well as its subject matter, made it very popular with American composers at the beginning of this century. But poems of symphonic effect, rather than those originated with the song-concept, are the ones which distinguish Lanier as an innovator, and so these are given emphasis here.

Paradoxically, music gave Lanier's poetry the qualities that cause it to be both admired and criticized. Music gave it life, rhythm, and rich texture, but many critics will point out that this texture is sometimes too rich, "lush," or "heavy"—too full of conscious attention to mellifluous sound. A phrase from *Sunrise* identifies the problem; Lanier's verses are sometimes "Over-sated with beauty" (l. 94). Perhaps he would have been able to "prune" his "luxuriance," as Bayard Taylor suggested, if he had had time.

It is for this very over-rich quality that Lanier's poetry is remembered and valued as an important development in American poetry. His experimentation in the mingling of sounds, in the exploitation of the possibilities of language, make him one of the most courageous and original of our poets. Like his beloved marshes, his poems are "beautiful-braided and woven / With intricate shades." His layered stages of sound, depicting the layers of nature—for nothing is seen that is not a combination of images, and nothing is heard that does not contain several sounds—represent the layers of our universe, some of which can be seen, some heard, and others only suggested.

CHAPTER XIV

An
Unfinished Symphony

And, ah, it haunts me just to know
His feet along these streets did go . . .
A haloed man—who also trod
The clouds around the throne of God. [1]

SIDNEY LANIER DIED on 7 September 1881 in the mountains of western North Carolina, a few miles from Asheville; it was his last refuge from tuberculosis. The severity of the disease during the previous winter had threatened to end his academic life; his orchestral days were already over. He had steadfastly refused to stop working, although, as Dr. Gilman recalled, he "gave his last lectures seated in a chair."[2] In the spring, hoping that mountain air could restore his strength, Lanier and his family moved south. In midsummer, he received a letter from Gilman, informing him of his reappointment as lecturer in English literature at Johns Hopkins; Lanier happily sent a letter of acceptance, but, too weak to hold a pen, he had to dictate it to Mary. To his last days, he continued to be character-

----

[1]Folger McKinsey, Baltimore poet, quoted in John Saulsbury Short, "Sidney Lanier, 'Familiar Citizen of the Town,' " 35 *Maryland Historical Magazine* (June 1940): 124.

[2]"Reminiscences of Sidney Lanier," *Pathfinder* (Sewanee TN) 1 (September 1906): 4.

istically optimistic, planning new books and artistic projects. Certainly his intellectual energy, as well as his musical exercise and the love of his family, enabled him to defy the disease as long as he did.

This man's struggle for recognition was even more difficult than his struggle to support his family, and the pressures of both often severely challenged his stubborn optimism. Only a very few individuals had a genuine appreciation of his art and understood all of the sacrifices that lay behind each poem. Yet, as in the case of others whose lives were similarly bitter, he became the object of adulation after his death. Praise of Lanier and his work, sometimes bordering on the extravagant, expectedly increased after 1881, and by 1888 English critic Edmund Gosse, in a disparaging article entitled "Has America Produced a Poet?" could note with disdain that this "idolatry" was "still on the increase."[3] From the 1880s through the 1940s, magazines and newspapers were filled with the words of Lanier's worshipers.

These approbations range from scholarly critiques of his work to ecstatic paeans bespeaking the existence of a virtual cult. The entire September 1906 issue of *The Pathfinder*, published at the University of the South, was dedicated "To the Memory of Sidney Lanier." In 1900 Harvey Smith McCowan wrote in the magazine entitled *Self-Culture* that when Lanier played "there emanated from him such a harmony of rhythm and beauty as could never be portrayed by laws of music alone."[4] McCowan also compared Lanier to the painter in one of Olive Schreiner's recently published *Dreams*; in this dream, called "The Artist's Secret," a painter creates mysteriously beautiful canvases, more wonderful than the creations of anyone else—because he paints with his own blood. He finally dies, and "it came to pass that after a while the artist was forgotten—but the work lived."[5] In 1926, Folger McKinsey, a Baltimore poet and writer, rhapsodized: "What rare wine they are missing who do not have some portion of [Lanier] every day to pick up, to commune with, to feel about afterward as if they had laid down something as intangible as a dawn and yet

---

[3]*Forum* (New York) 6 (October 1888): 180.

[4]*Self-Culture* (Akron OH) 10 (January 1900): 398.

[5]*Dreams* (Boston: Roberts Brothers, 1891) 119-20. Olive Schreiner (1855-1920) was a South African novelist and feminist.

as sure and abiding as human experience. . . . memories so dear to him as to be embalmed and sainted as though belonging to sacred dreams!"[6]

Much of this Lanier-worship took place in Baltimore. An early tribute from Baltimore friends, Mr. and Mrs. Lawrence Turnbull, is a commissioned painting by Annibale Gatti. This large canvas, painted in 1893, depicts the host of great poets mentioned in Lanier's *The Crystal*—Homer, Socrates, Dante, Shakespeare, Tennyson and others—all illumined by the radiant figure of Jesus above them.[7] Lanier is included in this poets' corner of heaven, between Tennyson and Browning.

Several commemorative ceremonies took place in Baltimore on the occasion of the anniversaries of the poet's birth. One such event was held at the Peabody concert hall on 4 February 1926; poet Lizette Woodworth Reese, speaking about "The Spirituality of Sidney Lanier," emphasized the parallel between his poetry and his life. "We fail to realize," she said, "that culture is inexorably bound up with character, with the cost of effort, ardent sacrifice, with the making of that hard fibre which is the stay of civilization. We need men of the spiritual type of Sidney Lanier to pull us up from what is below, to what is above."[8] The major address was delivered by the Reverend Oliver Huckel, who declared that Lanier was "Hellenic in his love of beauty . . . Hebraic in his passion for righteousness."[9] Several musical selections were played; two of these were performed by Lanier's old colleague, Frederick Gottlieb, who had joined the Peabody orchestra after Henry Wysham left Baltimore.

Others who knew Lanier recorded their memories in various journals. These individuals included Daniel Coit Gilman:

> Few men of letters in our land have left a more pathetic or a more inspiring record. Nothing could quench the poetic fire that burned within him. . . . Always cheerful, always gallant, always trustful—his presence

---

[6]"Lanier, Poet of Flute-Notes Clear and Always Clean," (Baltimore) *Evening Sun*, 4 February 1926.

[7]Aubrey Harrison Starke, *Sidney Lanier: A Biographical and Critical Study* (reprint, New York: Russell and Russell, 1964) 450, 496 n.22. The painting is now housed at the John Work Garrett Library, the Johns Hopkins University, Baltimore, Maryland.

[8]*Johns Hopkins Alumni Magazine* 14 (June 1926): 484.

[9]"Sidney Lanier Commemoration," ibid., 494.

in any company was quickening and inspiring. Let him enter a horse-car, and everyone was conscious that there was a man of mark; let him come upon the stage in a concert-room, a buzz would go through the audience; let him lecture, it was clear that he was one who would uphold the loftiest ideals.[10]

The Johns Hopkins University was the center of the major activity dedicated to Lanier, and over the years its alumni magazine has published many articles about him. One by Edwin Greenlaw in 1929 suggested the establishment of a "Sidney Lanier Professorship" at the university.[11] In 1893 Jacob Frey, a local historian, cited Baltimore's reputation as "the Monumental City" and complained that, other than a bust sculpted from life by Ephraim Keyser, there was no memorial to Lanier, "whose lines on Baltimore are quoted on platform and rostrum. . . . The naming of a library or public institution after him would be an appropriate honor."[12] In 1942, an impressive sculpture by Hans Schuler was unveiled at Johns Hopkins; here, outside the wall of the Homewood campus, an appropriately larger-than-life Sidney Lanier sits under the trees, pen and notebook in hand, his flute by his side, dreaming a new poem, oblivious to the traffic on North Charles Street. There are many other memorials to Lanier, in Georgia and North Carolina, but the one most vital is the collected edition of his works, published in 1945 by the Johns Hopkins University Press.

The people of Macon have done much to perpetuate the poet's fame. A committee led by Mrs. E. Dorothy Blount Lamar was influential, after the efforts of many years, in having him elected to the Hall of Fame at New York University in 1945. The Lanier home on High Street in Macon has been restored and opened as a historical site and the headquarters of the Middle Georgia Historical Society.

However, charm and gallantry, intensity and gentleness—as admirable as these attributes may be—are not sufficient to support an artistic reputation. The final analysis of Lanier as a poet and musician reveals that

[10]Daniel C. Gilman, "Pleasant Incidents of an Academic Life," *Scribner's* 31 (May 1902): 618.

[11]"A Sidney Lanier Professorship at Johns Hopkins," *Johns Hopkins Alumni Magazine* 17 (January 1929): 136-41.

[12]*Reminiscences of Baltimore* (Baltimore: Maryland Book Concern, 1893) 381.

he has endured because of more than his substantial talent. As a musician, he was praised both by friendly local critics and colleagues as well as by internationally known performers whose names are still familiar to music lovers. Lanier impressed Clara Louise Kellogg; Adelina Patti, another luminary of opera history, said of him: "He reveals to me a world of soul sweeter than music. I cannot sing; he has made my music smell musty."[13] Lanier has earned a sizable entry in *Grove's Dictionary of Music and Musicians* and is included in a recent *Biographical Dictionary of American Music*.[14] It is significant that several articles on Lanier in past years have been published in the musical journals *Etude* and *Musical Quarterly*. Admittedly, it has been many years since such articles have appeared in a music periodical, but a reviving interest in his compositions may produce additional contributions.

As a poet, he has suffered neglect since the 1940s, when the *Centennial Edition* appeared. In recent years, several new appraisals have been published,[15] and Lanier's poetry is still—but not always—included in new anthologies of poetry and American literature. Yet he remains on the periphery of our literature,[16] largely ignored by students. Rich, image-laden poetry, intertwined with philosophy, is not popular; an exemplary life is not inspiring; sentiment is an anachronism.

Yet Sidney Lanier continues to intrigue readers and critics who find in him a provoking originality; whatever the defects of his poetry, they are compensated by the freshness of thought and expression with which he

---

[13]Quoted in Aubrey Harrison Starke, "Sidney Lanier as a Musician," *Musical Quarterly* 20 (October 1934): 393.

[14]Charles Eugene Claghorn, *Biographical Dictionary of American Music* (West Nyack NY: Parker Publishing, 1973). Of the Baltimore group, only Lanier and Innes Randolph are mentioned.

[15]Jack DeBellis, *Sidney Lanier* (New York: Twayne, 1972); Lewis Leary, "The Forlorn Hope of Sidney Lanier," in *Southern Excursions: Essays on Mark Twain and Others* (Baton Rouge: Louisiana State University Press, 1971); Louis D. Rubin, Jr., "The Passion of Sidney Lanier," in *William Elliott Shoots a Bear: Essays on the Southern Literary Imagination* (Baton Route: Louisiana State University Press, 1976).

[16]Modern poets seem to have been affected very little by Lanier; only Richard Hovey acknowledges him as a direct influence, and today even Hovey is out of fashion.

approached his subjects. Lanier is an embodiment of courage, not only in his personal struggles, but in his artistic decisions as well. He chose to follow no school, no safe and established practices, no patterns except his own. It is this aesthetic integrity that has given his poetic voice its tone of individuality. He may have sung alone at times, but he was distinctly heard.

BIBLIOGRAPHY

PRIMARY SOURCES

Unpublished Letters

Asger Hamerik 1876, November 1. To Sidney Lanier, the Johns
Hopkins University (JHU)
1876, December 22. To Sidney Lanier, JHU
1877, December 12. To Sidney Lanier, JHU
1881, September 28. To Daniel C. Gilman, JHU

Mary Day Lanier 1870, December 12. To Sidney Lanier, JHU
1871, September 20. To Sidney Lanier, JHU
1878, April 15. To Robert S. Lanier, JHU

Sidney Lanier 1874, April 11. To Mary Day Lanier, JHU
1878, March 26. To Innes Randolph, JHU
1880, May 4. To William Hayes Ackland, the University
of North Carolina

Mina Mims 1903, February 25. To Henry W. Lanier, JHU

The Music of Sidney Lanier (Collection housed in the John Work Garrett Library,
the Johns Hopkins University)

Published Works

Little Ella, A Beautiful Ballad. Dedicated to Ella S. Montgomery by her friend S.
C. Lanier. Montgomery AL: R. W. Offutt, 1868.

Il Balen from *Il Trovatore.* Air and variation for Flute, with Piano Accompaniment, by the late Sidney Lanier. New Orleans: Badger, 1883.

A Little Song Gem. *Love That Hath Us in the Net.* Words by Tennyson; music by
Sidney Lanier. New Orleans: A. E. Blackmar, 1884.

Manuscripts (Most are undated; dates of composition are approximate)

The Song of Elaine (c. 1862); *Break, Break, Break* (c. 1871); *Flow Down, Cold Rivulet* (c. 1871); *Die Wacht Am Rhein* (1872); *The Song of the Lost Spirit* (1872); *Heimweh Polka* (1872); *Air for Symphony: Violin and Violoncello*; *A Sea Secret*; *Blackbirds* (fragment, c. 1873); *Wald-Einsamkeit*; *Wind-Song:* Flute solo (1874); *Symphony: Life* (fragments, c. 1881); *Blackbirds:* Solo for Flute (c. 1873); *Danse des Moucherons* (1873)—includes Lanier's programme for the piece on the dedication page.

The Charles D. Lanier and the Henry W. Lanier Collections at the Johns Hopkins University also contain the following items: programs of concerts in which Lanier performed; programs of concerts Lanier attended, or of which he was aware; the music collections of Sidney and Mary Day Lanier.

The papers of the Sutro Collection of the Maryland Historical Society include Books of Records of the Wednesday Club, 1869-1886, and the Club Scrapbook.

SECONDARY SOURCES

Abrams, M. H. et al., eds. *Norton Anthology of English Literature.* New York: W. W. Norton, 1968, vol. 1.

Anderson, Charles R. et al., eds. *The Centennial Edition of the Works of Sidney Lanier.* 10 vols. Baltimore: Johns Hopkins University Press, 1945.

Apthorp, W. F. "The Centennial Cantata." *Dwight's Journal of Music.* 8 July 1876: 261.

Baltimore City Directory and Ladies Visiting and Shopping Guide. Baltimore: W. H. Durfee, 1878.

Baskervill, William Malone. *Southern Writers: Biographical and Critical Studies: Sidney Lanier.* Nashville: Barbee and Smith, 1896.

Beirne, Francis F. *Baltimore . . . a picture history, 1858-1968.* Baltimore: Bodine and Associates, 1968.

Bennett, Joseph. "The Poetic Basis of Music." *Dwight's Journal of Music.* 2 May 1874: 217-19.

Blom, Eric, ed. *Grove's Dictionary of Music and Musicians.* 5th ed. London: Macmillan, 1954.

Bode, Carl. *Antebellum Culture.* Carbondale: Southern Illinois University Press, 1970.

Brown, Calvin S. *Music and Literature: A Comparison of the Arts.* Athens: University of Georgia Press, 1948.

Bulling, George T. "Poets and Composers of Music." *Dwight's Journal of Music.* 25 May 1878: 233-34.

Butler, John C. *Historical Record of Macon and Central Georgia.* Macon: J. W. Burke, 1879.

Chase, Gilbert. *America's Music: From the Pilgrims to the Present.* Revised, 2d ed. New York: McGraw-Hill, 1966.

Claghorn, Charles Eugene. *Biographical Dictionary of American Music.* West Nyack NY: Parker Publishing, 1973.

Claus, Linda. "A Style Analysis of the 'Nordische Suite' of Asger Hamerik." M.A. thesis, Peabody Conservatory of Music, 1975.

DeBellis, Jack. *Sidney Lanier.* New York: Twayne, 1972.

Dobbin, Isabel L. "Lanier at the Peabody." *Peabody Bulletin.* April-May 1911: 4-5.

"Editor's Literary Record." *Harper's* 61 (October 1880): 796-97.

Ewen, David. *Music Comes to America.* New York: Thomas Y. Crowell, 1942.

Fletcher, John Gould. "Sidney Lanier." *The University of Kansas City Review* 16 (Winter 1949).

Foster, Stephen Collins. *Songs and Compositions.* Produced by the staff of Foster Hall, Walter R. Whittlesey et al. Indianapolis: Foster Hall Reproductions, 1933.

Franklin, Benjamin. "Quartet, three violins and violoncello, F major." Performed by members of the Royal Philharmonic, London. New York: Society for the Preservation of the American Musical Heritage, 1965.

French, John C. *A History of the University Founded by Johns Hopkins.* Baltimore: Johns Hopkins University Press, 1946.

————. "Sidney Lanier's Life in Baltimore." (Baltimore) *Sun.* 6 September 1931.

Frey, Jacob. *Reminiscences of Baltimore.* Baltimore: Maryland Book Concern, 1893.

Gilman, Daniel Coit. "The Launching of a University." *Scribner's* 31 (March 1902): 327-36.

————. "Pleasant Incidents of an Academic Life." *Scribner's* 31 (May 1902): 614-24.

————. "Reminiscences of Sidney Lanier." *The Pathfinder* 1 (September 1906): 2-5.

Gosse, Edmund. "Has America Produced a Poet?" *Forum* (New York) 6 (October 1880).

Gottlieb, Frederick H. "Sidney Lanier." (Copy, unpublished address.) Charles D. Lanier Papers, the Johns Hopkins University, Baltimore, Maryland.

Graham, Philip. "A Note on Lanier's Music." *University of Texas Studies in English* 17 (1937): 107-11.

Greenlaw, Edwin. "A Sidney Lanier Professorship at Johns Hopkins." *The Johns Hopkins Alumni Magazine* 17 (January 1929): 136-41.

Higgins, Richard. "Sidney Lanier, Musician." Ph.D. dissertation, Peabody Conservatory of Music, 1969.

Higginson, Thomas Wentworth. "Sidney Lanier." *Chautauquan* 7 (April 1887): 416-18.

Hitchcock, H. Wiley. *Music in the United States: An Introduction.* Englewood Cliffs: Prentice-Hall, 1969.

Hopkins, G. M. *City Atlas of Baltimore, Maryland and environs, from official records, private plans and actual surveys, based upon plans deposited in the Department of Surveys;* surveyed & published under the direction of G. M. Hopkins. Philadelphia: G. M. Hopkins, 1876.

Howard, John Tasker, and George Kent Bellows. *A Short History of Music in America.* New York: Thomas Y. Crowell, 1957.

Hubbell, Jay B. *The South in American Literature: 1607-1900.* Durham: Duke University Press, 1964.

Illing, Robert. *A Dictionary of Music.* Baltimore: Penguin, 1950.

Jacob, Kathryn A. "1876: Marking—and Making—History." *Johns Hopkins Magazine* 26 (September 1975): 10-20.

Keefer, Lubov. *Baltimore's Music: The Haven of the American Composer.* Baltimore: J. H. Furst, 1962.

Kellogg, Clara Louise. *Memoirs of an American Prima Donna.* New York: G. P. Putnam's Sons, 1913.

Kelly, Frederick. "Sidney Lanier at the Peabody Institute." *Peabody Bulletin* (1939): 35-38.

Lanier, Clifford A. "Reminiscences of Sidney Lanier." *Chautauquan* 21 (July 1895): 403-409.

———. "Sidney Lanier." *Gulf States Historical Magazine* (July 1903).

Leach, Joseph. *Bright Particular Star: The Life and Times of Charlotte Cushman.* New Haven: Yale University Press, 1970.

Leary, Lewis. "The Forlorn Hope of Sidney Lanier." In *Southern Excursions: Essays on Mark Twain and Others.* Baton Rouge: Louisiana State University Press, 1971.

Leichentritt, Hugo. *Music, History, and Ideas.* Cambridge: Harvard University Press, 1938.

Lenhart, Charmenz S. *Musical Influence on American Poetry.* Athens: University of Georgia Press, 1956.

Litz, Francis A. *Father Tabb.* Baltimore: Johns Hopkins University Press, 1923.

Long, Francis Taylor. "The Life of Richard Malcolm Johnston in Maryland." *Maryland Historical Magazine* 34 (December 1939): 305-24.

Macfarren, G. A. "The Pictorial Power of Music." *Dwight's Journal of Music* (24 July 1875): 1.

McCauley, Louis B. *Maryland Historical Prints: A Selection from the Robert G. Merrick Collection, Maryland Historical Society, and Other Maryland Collections.* Baltimore: Maryland Historical Society, 1975.

McCowan, Harvey Smith. "Sidney Lanier, the Southern Singer and His Songs." *Self-Culture* 10 (January 1900): 398-400.

Malone, Kemp. "Sidney Lanier." *The Johns Hopkins Alumni Magazine* 21 (March 1933): 244-49.

Mayfield, John S. "Sidney Lanier in Texas." *Texas Monthly* (December 1928): 650-67.

Mims, Edwin. *Sidney Lanier.* New York: Houghton, Mifflin, 1905.

Monrad-Johansen, David. *Edvard Grieg.* Translated from the Norwegian by Madge Robertson. Reprint. New York: Tudor Publishing, 1945.

Mussulman, Joseph A. *Music in the Cultured Generation: A Social History of Music in America, 1870-1900.* Evanston: Northwestern University Press, 1971.

Niecks, Frederick. *Programme Music in the Last Four Centuries.* London: Novello, 1907.

Ortmann, Otto. "Musical Baltimore in the Seventies." (Baltimore) *Evening Sun.* 8, 16 July 1935.

Peabody Institute. *Seventh Annual Report of the Provost to the Trustees.* 4 June 1874.

_____. *Twelfth Annual Report of the Provost to the Trustees.* 1 June 1879.

_____. "Sidney Lanier: Program of a Meeting Held in the Concert Hall of the Peabody Institute on February 3, 1940."

Pratt, Waldo Selden, ed. *Grove's Dictionary of Music and Musicians, American Supplement* (6). Philadelphia: Theodore Presser, 1927.

Randel, William Peirce. *Centennial: American Life in 1876.* New York: Chilton, 1969.

Reese, Lizette Woodworth. "The Spirituality of Sidney Lanier." *The Johns Hopkins Alumni Magazine* 14 (June 1926): 482-84.

Remington, Miss, comp. *Society Visiting List for the Season of 1890-91.* Baltimore: Guggenheimer, Weil, 1890.

Rhys, Ernest, ed. *Prose and Poetry by Heinrich Heine.* New York: E. P. Dutton, 1934.

Robinson, Ray Edward. *The Peabody Conservatory: An American Solution to a European Musical Philosophy.* 2 vols. Baltimore: Peabody Conservatory, 1968.

Roquie, Margaret B. "Sidney Lanier, Poet-Musician." *The Etude* 55 (September 1937): 576, 617.

Rubin, Louis D., Jr. "The Passion of Sidney Lanier." In *William Elliott Shoots a Bear: Essays on the Southern Literary Imagination.* Baton Rouge: Louisiana State University Press, 1976.

Sablosky, Irving. *American Music.* Chicago: University of Chicago Press, 1969.

Schreiner, Olive. *Dreams.* Boston: Roberts Brothers, 1891.

Short, John Saulsbury. "Sidney Lanier, 'Familiar Citizen of the Town.' " *Maryland Historical Magazine* 35 (June 1940): 121-46.

Spiller, Robert E. *The Oblique Light: Studies in Literary History and Biography.* New York: Macmillan, 1948.

Starke, Aubrey H. "An Omnibus of Poets." *The Colophon* 4, pt. 16. New York: The Colophon, 1934.

————. *Sidney Lanier: A Biographical and Critical Study.* Chapel Hill: University of North Carolina Press, 1933. Reprint. New York: Russell and Russell, 1964.

————. "Sidney Lanier as a Musician." *Musical Quarterly* 20 (October 1934): 384-400.

Stein, Jack M. *Richard Wagner and the Synthesis of the Arts.* Detroit: Wayne State University Press, 1960.

Stieff, Frederick Philip. "Music in Baltimore." *Art and Archaeology* 19 (June 1925): 255-58.

Stokes, I[saac] N[ewton] Phelps. *New York, Past and Present.* New York: Plantin Press, 1939.

Sutro, Ottilie. "The Wednesday Club: A Brief Sketch from Authentic Sources." *Maryland Historical Magazine* 38 (March 1943): 60-68.

Taylor, C. B. *One Hundred Years' Achievements of a Free People.* New York: Henry S. Allen, 1876.

Thomas, Theodore. *A Musical Autobiography.* Edited by George P. Upton. 2 vols. Chicago: A. C. McClung, 1905.

Upton, William Treat. *Art-Song in America: A Study in the Development of American Music.* Boston: Oliver Ditson, 1930.

Vexler, Robert I., comp. and ed. *Baltimore: A Chronological and Documentary History, 1632-1970.* Dobbs Ferry NY: Oceana Publications, 1975.

White, Edward Lucas. "Reminiscences of Sidney Lanier." *The Johns Hopkins Alumni Magazine* 17 (June 1929): 329-31.

INDEX

MUP *A Living Minstrelsy*

Designed by Margaret Jordan Brown
Composition by MUP Composition Department

Production specifications:
    text paper—60-pound Warren's Olde Style
    endpapers—Multicolor Antique Ash Grey
    covers (on .088 boards)—Holliston Roxite B 53596
    dust jacket—100-pound enamel printed 2 colors—
        PMS 416 (grey) and PMS 485 (red)

Printing (offset lithography) and binding
    by Penfield-Rowland Printing Company, Inc., Macon, Georgia